North Se...
Requiem aeternam dona eis (Rest eternal grant unto them)

A tribute to those 20th Century professional divers who lost their lives whilst playing their part in effecting the extraction of oil and gas from the North Sea, 1971-1999.

About the Author

Jim Limbrick was born in Deal, Kent, where except for two years in Wales he spent his formative years before joining the Royal Navy at Gosport, Hampshire, as a Boy Seaman at the age of 15 years. By the age of 19 he was a qualified Navy diver. On honourably completing his service time he left the Navy to take up various civilian positions as a diver, and as a diver/navigator on oil exploration projects around the world.

After working in the North Sea in its early years, he settled with a diving company in the Middle East where he worked as a diver on some of the world's largest oil-field installation projects of the time. He later supervised and then managed divers engaged on oil-field installation, inspection, and maintenance diving operations, on contract to the largest oil company in that part of the world.

He returned to Deal in 1978, taking over the reins of his angling charter business and working full time in Local Government until retirement, moving to Norfolk in 1988. He has been happily associated with diving and divers in one way or another, latterly through old friends and colleagues, for the last 46 years, and though he has known *some* sad and bad times within the business, overall he nevertheless regrets not one single day of it, and in recommending the profession to any young man today, Jim's only regret is that he cannot do it all over again.

Published by New Generation Publishing in 2016
Copyright © Jim Limbrick 2016
All photos © Jeff Taylor & Jim Limbrick

The author asserts the moral right under the Copyright, Designs and Patents Act 1988 to be identified as the author of this work.

All Rights reserved. No part of this publication may be reproduced, stored in a retrieval system or transmitted, in any form or by any means without the prior consent of the author, nor be otherwise circulated in any form of binding or cover other than that which it is published and without a similar condition being imposed on the subsequent purchaser.

ISBN: 978-1-78719-098-6

www.newgeneration-publishing.com

New Generation Publishing

North Sea Divers-a Requiem

by

Jim Limbrick

Preface

Within the pages of this book I have personally expressed an earnest wish to pay tribute to those professional divers in the North European oil and gas industry, mainly the North Sea, who lost their lives in playing their part in effecting the extraction of those very important hydrocarbons. I hoped at best to convey that tribute by profiling these men as real people rather than as statistics, along with some detail of their personal lives and former lifetime achievements. However, with what information I have so far been able to gather, for reasons to do with comparatively poor methods of record keeping in past years compared to to-days computer databases, what you see is what I have. Not the fault of office staff of years gone by I hasten to add; our modern types of recording systems were just not available to them.

At this stage I have not wanted to approach relatives, friends, or former colleagues of the deceased divers, certainly not those of relatively recent bereavement. But I hope that one day they will voluntarily come to me, when they will be greatly welcomed, as then perhaps we can jointly produce an up to date, definitive historical record of the men who died; their personalities, their interests, families and friends, and perhaps some photographs, when all of whom, and their descendants, can look back with pride on some of the very important achievements in the oil and gas industry of which these men were an essential part.

I am, at present, left only with some sets of facts and figures and Government statistics, resulting in a situation where I can only tell, as shown in the chapters preceding the list of fatalities, what sort of things the divers were likely to have been involved in, no matter where their diving location, at home or overseas, and then relate how it is documented that they met their fatal ends. A very sombre and harrowing subject, and a very sad one, especially for those who lost loved ones over the years, but I want those divers' contributions to be known to all, as a true historical record of brave lives lost during one of the 20th Century's most momentous periods of the United Kingdom's latter day Industrial Revolution.

I want their loved ones to know this too, that they did not die in vain, as on the occasion of any such death the cases brought forth new recommendations or legislation on safety matters to the benefit of all those following behind. I will show some of these when I itemise each fatality, and I hope that friends and relatives of our brave departed divers will draw some comfort and consolation from them.

This book is written for the understanding of the interested general public, not as a diving or safety manual update for those already in the know. I do not pretend for one moment, having been out of diving for a good many years, that I am personally fully conversant with all that has been written here about modern day diving and diving methods, but a genuine effort has been made to present facts to a public with little or no knowledge of the various aspects of the whole subject matter so that they may more readily understand what goes on where divers go to work. I have had to rely a great deal on information obtained from many sources, in addition to my own knowledge and experiences, but my only thought throughout has been that the divers mentioned herein will not be forgotten for all that they contributed.

Constructive criticism, rather than negative comment, is always welcome, as there is most always something, somewhere, that is not quite right in the written non-fiction word, though I feel quite certain that writers generally do their very best in honestly presenting the facts as known to them; which is what I have done.

Any comment forthcoming in that respect would hopefully serve to further the cause of the possibility of the definitive version of all the events mentioned herein, coupled with complete detail on technical matters, being published in full; which is my dearest wish.

Jim Limbrick

Norfolk, England

Contents

The Divers,	1
The Oil And Gas,	13
Getting It Out Of The Ground,	23
Offshore Life (and Death),	27
The Good Old Bad Old Days,	33
The Right Stuff,	44
It Has To Be The Money,	49
A Bit Of Theory,	55
Some Technicalities,	63
THE FATALITIES,	80
Changes in Diving Regulations	184
Health and Safety - the Future	187
Unions	189
Useful Addresses	192
Acknowledgements	194

Chapter One

THE DIVERS

Many books and articles have been written about that near God forsaken piece of the North Atlantic Ocean, the North Sea. It lies to the east of the British Isles and its eastern boundaries from north to south are the coasts of Norway, Denmark, Germany, the Netherlands and Belgium.

A brief return journey north through this valuable piece of marine real estate takes us from the bottle-neck of the Dover Straits in the south, up through the rich gas fields of the Leman Bank off Bacton in Norfolk, stretching on up to fields off Teeside, and continuing on up through a vast sea of empty space before reaching the great Forties Field off Aberdeen and Peterhead. Its multitude of neighbouring fields, from Clyde in the south to Harding to the north, can be clearly seen on a fine day with their oil and gas platforms standing starkly against the iron grey daylight sky, or the flickering candle-like gas flares turning night skies into day.

On then past Orkney and the huge Frigg gas field and its smaller satellites, and ever further north to the East Shetland Basin and its huge conglomerate of gas and oilfields. And venturing yet further north beyond these where within the exceedingly hostile environment of the northern North Sea lies the Magnus oilfield, and the ocean begins to widen eastwards to meet with the extensive expanse of the Norwegian Sea, reaching on up to the Arctic Circle where, commencing in November each year, the days will turn slowly into one long night for the full three months duration of the dark Arctic winter.

To the west of Shetland in the Faroes/Shetland Trough lie the Foinaven and Schiehallion fields in the UK's deepest exploited water to date, with the Clair oilfield, the largest undeveloped field in the North Sea, seemingly acting as buffer between them and Shetland.

The North Sea is a huge expanse of deep, cold, and often stormy water extending to more than half a million square kilometres (over 200,000 square miles) and over 650 metres (2,100 feet) at its deepest, where fierce winter gales create mountainous, foaming and ever changing grey green to black, white topped seas, and where man, both above and below the water, goes precariously about the business of searching for and extracting the hydrocarbons which were formed millions of years ago far beneath the seabed of those icy waters, and which have been so vitally important to the United Kingdom of Great Britain's energy needs for our light, heat, and mobility over the last twenty five years, with the oil alone accounting for around one third of our energy consumption.

Though we occasionally hear or read something of the durable, tenacious and resilient people who are gainfully employed in these waters, and diving films and books by the hundred on clear blue still water, coral reefs and multi-coloured fish are much in abundance, let us stop for a moment and consider the commercial realities rather than the leisure and recreational side of underwater life where, to my knowledge, nothing in detail has been written about the men who went to work beneath those dark, cold, and fast running deep waters, and lost their lives whilst doing so.

The North Sea has been the United Kingdom's point of focus for oil and gas exploration and production since the mid 1960's, and the list of known diving fatalities in oil and gas operations in Northern Europe from that time to the end of the 20th century has been a most shocking 58 divers of various nationalities - all in the North Sea but for a few exceptions, and the majority of them British; but also Norwegian, American, French, Dutch and Italian.

Brave, perceptive and resourceful men, and vitally important, indeed essential, to the success of the construction and ongoing maintenance of oil and gas installations, and the subsequent extraction of their products which vastly benefit the UK economy and the country's export figures as a whole.

Leading precarious offshore lives aboard "petrol factories" and facing possible death on a daily basis, strong minded and individualistic, they generally worked as a single man unit underwater, but came together in a team when required in a way most people requiring team spirit amongst their employees would envy. These were men who were exceedingly optimistic about their lives, who thought their futures were assured, and all of whom challenged those underwater conditions for their livelihoods, only to lose those lives in the prime of their existence.

As in war they were basically young men, most all with wives, children and girlfriends, and most certainly families, friends and relatives. Men whom I hope to ensure will never be forgotten for what they accomplished, the legacy they left us, and the fact that they were so very colourful, so much larger than life and, some of them, my friends and colleagues.

That exceedingly courageous, resolute, good humoured, and somewhat eccentric mixed bunch of often totally outrageous characters, professional divers, are drawn from all classes of society and all quarters of the globe and, perhaps unusually, many of them from all kinds of previous different professions who, for reasons best known to themselves, decided to make diving their newly chosen vocation. Not entirely rejecting their former way of life, but seeking out those companies the length and breadth of the world who would pay them well to utilise their hard-earned skills and experience, sometimes in foreign oil and gas fields, but most certainly in our own, to fulfil our nation's increasing reliance on the products of those skills. Seamen, airmen, soldiers, coal miners, accountants, building workers, university graduates, shop assistants, naval and army officers, or farm-workers; it seems to matter not in the least in the initiative these men have taken to

Pipeline riser and dog-leg

improve their lifestyle by investing in their futures. To earn more money, of course, but sometimes just as importantly to do something they consider rather more worthwhile and considerably more interesting than that in which they were perhaps previously gainfully employed.

Select numbers of divers end up in the oilfield business because it is, without doubt, a very serious business, but a great and fascinating adventure too. To be a vital part of the exploration for, or production of, oil and gas in what must surely be, more often than not, one of the most interesting jobs in the world can be nothing short of a huge bonus in a profession dearly loved, with a passion that people who dislike or are indifferent towards the water would find exceedingly hard to understand.

Not exactly on a par with astronauts walking on the moon, or changing out a computer on the Hubble Telescope, but nevertheless, when major goals are achieved, it often seems just as fantastic, considering that the underwater world is still almost as totally alien to man as it was a million years ago, even though our seas cover about seventy percent of the earth's surface.

I can well remember diving in an attempt to stab the then world's largest oil pipeline riser (the pipe which brings oil up from the seabed) of 142 centimetres (56 inches) in diameter, and weighing around 120 tonnes, into the 'tube turn' (the bend as the pipeline turns up from the seabed to rise up a platform) of a pipeline at the base of a platform on Kharg Island in Iran. It was only in about twenty eight metres (ninety feet) of water but dangling precariously on the end of a crane wire, so when it finally went in and lined up, after many round the clock previous attempts by the whole diving team, it was like all your Christmas's had come on the same day.

In the very early days of North Sea operations many divers were drawn from their respective native shores of the two most productive countries bordering the North Sea - Britain and Norway. But others arrived in our prospective and budding gas and oilfields on rigs, boats, helicopters, and offshore barges, from countries as diverse as Germany, Holland, Italy and France, to South and East Africa and Australia. And not a few from the United States of America, and other Mediterranean island countries too, such as Malta, Greece and Cyprus, to mention just some of the cosmopolitan mix of nationalities, some of which to this day, as in many other oilfield skills, blend seamlessly within the three percent of non-European Union nationals employed throughout the offshore industry, who are gladly absorbed within the industry as a whole for their welcome and valued skills.

Though generally on good terms with what they do, divers have their good and bad days like anyone else, but are rarely heard to state that they would rather be doing something different, notwithstanding all the hardships and dangers they are often called upon to endure. Money aside, in the final analysis they still very much like the job they are doing, and great confidence in their own abilities is one of their major assets, whether that be applied to the physical side of diving, the profession as a whole, or to any other aspect of their lives.

Most all, and quite naturally so, would readily agree that the money they can earn is the primary incentive and, if successfully trained at one of the schools for professional divers, or leaving the Armed Forces as a trained diver and getting offshore certification, will attempt to enter the oil-field business at the very first opportunity, as that is where the big money is.

Some will be disappointed as it is not a situation one can just walk into. It's a bit of a 'Catch 22' situation where, even with the appropriate training and certification, hands-on previous experience can sometimes be the order of the day and, without that experience, jobs can still be hard to come by unless, of course, you have proven ability - perhaps a good spell in civil engineering or dockyard diving - and strong powers of persuasion.

No matter what profession a person is considering entering, and diving is no different, actually getting a job with a diving company depends a great deal on the applicant's ability to interest a prospective employer in his previous experience and the qualifications that he has obtained. He would have to prove his ability enough to persuade that employer that he will be a reliable employee, fit and able to undertake any reasonably required task, be a credit and an asset to the company, and be amenable to the employers' required working routine. He will also have to assure the employer of his availability for work at a moment's notice, a great deal of which will be unsocial hours, and will include days such as Christmas and other Bank Holidays, and possibly include much time away from home, perhaps for weeks or even months at a time. He will, of course, subsequently need to prove that he can work as a cohesive member of a team. Although the average professional diver is something of a special individual, there is no place for individuals in the context of the kind of teamwork required in the diving business.

Without doubt the UK offers some of the best, if not *the* best, commercial diver training in the world; some training companies having many years of experience, and with the most recognised qualifications in the field of Commercial Diving to be obtained anywhere. At first glance the cost of the various courses may seem prohibitive but when you consider what you get for your money, and how quickly you can earn it back again at a basic £200 a day plus, once gainfully employed offshore, it can only be looked upon as one of the best investments an interested person could make. Invariably an aptitude test will need to be taken, and this is in everyone's interest, as you the budding diver will not want to waste your money if you are not really suited to the industry, and the diving schools don't want you if you are not cut out for the job. They are experts at assessing this in a very short space of time. Many applicants fail right there, and some fail on the course, and even more leave the industry very quickly when they find out at first hand that life for the average diver is not always the glamorous bed of roses they imagined it would be, but instead is one with much repetitive, boring, dangerous, and dirty work.

Once a diver has some basic air training and a suitable qualification, to gain some good open water experience, those shallower and less demanding oilfields of the Middle East or South America are recommended as good training grounds before applying for training to obtain the necessary offshore certification, and making what can only be classed as a major transition to the likes of the North Sea.

It is almost certain that initially the new diver will find more work opportunities abroad than in the UK, and often better pay too, probably because in total there's a lot more going on worldwide, plus the fact that most diving companies abroad now require HSE (Health and Safety Executive) certificated divers to at least Units A and B (old Part 3) standard, as shown below, as older, less qualified divers are phased out; mostly on a voluntary basis. This is no doubt due to the fact that the relevant divisions of many foreign countries around the world are becoming members of the International Marine Contractors Association and are insisting on HSE standards. Without doubt the UK has been responsible for the implementation of safer diving practises worldwide and the perhaps unwitting ambassadorship abroad of our well qualified and competent divers and supervisors has shown the world the way, putting them in great demand; and that is very commendable.

Like some other professions, qualified divers are not tested specifically for diving ability or knowledge before going to work on a particular job but they must, of course, be fully qualified and medically approved for the particular type of diving work they want to do, and be able to produce certification to that effect. And when they get to a diving location it will very soon be established whether or not they are suited to the job and, just as importantly, show a willingness to fit in as a good, knowledgeable and reliable member of a team. The industry having recognised the importance of the diving supervisor has made him entirely responsible for, amongst many other things, seeing that this is the case. He will check that all and any diver on his team will be fit and well, suitably qualified and competent to carry out the work required to be done on a specific site, and fully certificated for such work with the certificate in his possession. That doesn't mean to say that you have to be totally conversant with all aspects of the job from day one as you are brought on through the system, dependent on your increasing experience, and given appropriate duties in which you will be ably assisted and encouraged by all members of the team.

In the UK there are various categories of certificated diver, (see table below), the main two of which concerning the offshore industry are the Surface Supplied (Top Up) and the Mixed Gas, or Closed Bell diver. A closed bell is a dry bell, used usually on lengthy mixed gas surface oriented or 'saturation' work (see page 68), as opposed to a wet bell which, as its name certainly implies, is open sided to the water. This wet bell, like its closed bell brother, is fitted with its own independent life-support system should there be any problem with continuity of the main surface supplies, and is used for dives of relevantly short duration using natural air or mixed gas, depending on depth.

The industry safe accepted depth limit for surface supplied air diving is up to 50 metres (165 feet), and for the 'Top Up' diver mentioned, this is the advanced air diving qualification allowing a diver to work offshore using all types of air diving equipment and techniques which include wet bells and hot water suits. The diver will be thoroughly trained and certificated in all aspects of the hardware of air diving, and methods of decompression, along with First Aid training, which is compulsory, and have a working knowledge of diving physiology.

Closed Bell Mixed Gas Diving, as discussed later, is an obtainable skill for which qualified divers with at least one year of certificated offshore experience and at least 50 hours of logged dives to various water depths, will present themselves at the gates

This Saturation system is containerised

of a suitable diving school for this advanced and intensive course, which trains a diver to work to unlimited depths using oxygen and helium breathing mixtures on saturation diving techniques, and be a top man in his field. However, it is recommended by some who have gone this route that it is probably better to get rather *more* than one year of working experience before making application.

UK diving schools played a major role in training many of the early oilfield divers, and have been instrumental over the years in helping to improve overall safety in the offshore diving industry.

In addition to the schools' speciality courses in underwater systems and training, divers can obtain additional skills such as underwater welding, cutting and burning, and non destructive testing or, importantly, qualify as a 'Diver Medic' as, under offshore diving legislation, every offshore diving team must have at least one such qualified person. One particular centre in the UK is universally recognised as the world leader in Commercial Diver

Training, and offers HSE certification for working divers within the UK, as well as equivalent certification overseas.

The United States of America does not have a Government diver certification scheme, but anyone undertaking and completing a diving course at one of the United States diver training schools stands a good chance of obtaining work over there. However, that person then needs to consider how that will affect him getting work in UK waters at some time in the distant future, as to dive commercially anywhere in the UK you do need that HSE certification, or its accepted equivalent, and this does not include USA diving school certificates. No matter what kind of professional diving you intend to do, both in the UK and many countries overseas where diving companies are members of The International Marine Contractors Association, whether inshore or offshore, you do need that important piece of paper. At present overseas certification is accepted by the HSE from Australia, Canada, South Africa, and most European countries.

Many young men, who are to be encouraged, and must be over the age of 18 years to actually be employed offshore as a diver in the UK, will perhaps start off as 'tenders'. In other words, getting employment around docks and harbours, or other civil engineering type work, tending to divers' needs with a view to becoming a diver themselves one day.

Although in general there are no actual diver apprenticeship schemes available, these eager, nascent divers can be employed, under supervision, dressing and undressing divers in their diving suits and ancillary equipment, washing out and looking after the equipment after dives, tending lines and hoses, setting up and cleaning dive stations, checking chambers, taking care of and checking compressors, fuel and oil levels, draining filters, and making sure compressor exhaust fumes, or any other kind of bad air from any source, are not likely to cause death or danger by getting sucked into the diver's air supply. They can generally make themselves useful around the diving scene in addition to thoroughly familiarising themselves with every aspect of the operation, just as the divers and everyone else connected to the operation, will know so to do. Not least they should be familiar with any diving procedure to be used, along with contingency plans for any arising emergency.

The better tenders may actually be qualified divers, but so limited in experience that they will probably be employed in the capacity of tender before being 'broken out' by a kindly inshore supervisor.

The job of tender is a composite and important one, and should not be underestimated in its importance for gaining experience towards the ultimate goal of qualifying as a fully certificated diver and going on to greater things, or actually being asked to make a straightforward first operational dive if already qualified.

Some people make a specific career as a diving tender, with no intention of ever going under the water, though this is found more on the Civil Engineering side of things. In the USA where the tender system is most common, some freelance divers employ their own permanent tender, the latter looking after his master in all things connected with the diver's work, equipment and well-being when they are at work, and sometimes acting as a general dogs-body when they are not. In these cases the diver pays the tender out of his own earnings, and they are, and act, as a team.

However, none of the above relieves the person actually about to carry out a dive of his own ultimate responsibility in checking that everything to be used in connection with his dive is in order, nor the whole team in fact, as it is incumbent upon them to carry out pre-dive checks on all the plant and equipment no matter how much reliance is generally placed on the fact that it was in order the day, or even the dive, before.

In the UK, the Diving Operations at Work Regulations 1997, make it mandatory that all working divers be qualified to the appropriate HSE approved standard for the type of diving operations which they will be undertaking, and in addition that they must keep a daily record or diving log of each dive specifically detailing such things as their diving contractor employer's name and address, date of dive, dive location, personal diving equipment used, depth of dive, bottom time, work undertaken, any subsequent decompression details, and any problems that may have arisen. This list is by no means definitive, and were I a budding diver today, or even a well qualified one with supervisory ambition who wanted to refresh his memory and prepare himself for advancement, in addition to obtaining a copy of "The Professional Diver's Handbook", I would consider the current purchase price of the Approved Code of Practice an exceedingly good overall investment for *all* that it contains in being approved for the purposes of providing practical guidance with respect to the requirements of the above Regulations.

From 1981 to 1998 these were the Standards for Assessing Diver Competence:
Part 1   Basic Air Diving
Part 11   Mixed Gas diving
Part 111   Air Diving where no surface compression chamber is required on site.
Part 1V   Air Diving with Self-Contained Equipment where no surface compression chamber is required on site.

From 1998 onwards, Health and Safety Diver Competences are:
Unit A   Surface Supplied Diving-
Assessed to dive to a maximum depth of 50 metres (165 feet), (not less than 40 metres). Can work to 50 metres.
Unit B   SCUBA Diving-
Assessed to dive to a maximum depth of 30 metres (100 feet), (not less than 25 metres). Can work to 50 metres. (This anomaly is correct).
Unit C   Closed Bell Diving-
A pre-requisite for this type of diving is that the diver must have HSE Surface Supplied and Surface Supplied (Top Up) Diving qualifications or accepted equivalents, and a minimum 12 months offshore experience, including dives to various depths. Assessed to dive to 100 metres on a combined bounce/saturation dive profile. (See page 66).
Unit D   Surface Supplied Diving (Top-Up).
For this type of diving the diver must have an HSE Surface Supplied Diving qualification or an accepted equivalent. Assessment is on three topics: use of a wet bell; use of hot water suits; and theory of the hazards involved in diving from a Dynamically Positioned vessel. (See pages 72 & 178). A diver cannot work offshore in the air range unless he holds the HSE Surface Supplied and Surface Supplied (Top Up) Diving qualifications, or accepted equivalents.

The older type certificates issued under the Diving Operations at Work Regulations 1981 are still valid, as are transitional certificates issued under regulation 15 of these regulations, and certificates issued by the Manpower Services Commission and the Training Services Agency. Further and fuller explanations of these titles are obtainable from the HSE (Offshore Division, Diving Operations Strategy Team) in London, or any British Diver Training Centre.

All divers working in the UK also require a certificate of medical fitness to dive, and the HSE Guidance to "Medical Examiners of Divers" Form MA1 outlines the HSE medical standards for diving at work. These are used by medical examiners approved by the HSE to perform statutory diving medical examinations and assessments under the Diving at Work Regulations 1997.

Form MA1 is a comprehensive twelve-page document, and it is highly recommended within that document that anyone considering a career in diving should complete a medical questionnaire obtainable from the HSE, or a diver-training organisation offering competence assessment leading to the award of a qualification approved by the HSE. This questionnaire looks at whether anything in a person's medical history would preclude them from a career in diving, which they can check with their own GP, thus saving on time and expense for all concerned.

Within the next year the HSE will have stopped approving medical examiners of divers outside of the UK. However, a programme of mutual recognition of European Member State diving medicals is being progressed by the HSE, who already have mutual recognition with Norway.

Chapter Two

THE OIL AND GAS

The openings for such adventurers were formulated in the early to mid 1960s when natural gas, a mixture of ethane and methane, was first discovered in the North Sea. Major production has continued there since 1967, and the first major oil finds were made in 1969/70, in both the Norwegian and UK sectors - the Norwegian Ekofisk Fields, and the now exceedingly well known UK Forties Field, with its 169 kilometres (105 miles) long by 92 centimetres (36 inches) diameter pipeline to Cruden Bay on the north east coast of Scotland. This traverses by way of the unmanned BP 'Unity Riser' five kilometres to the west of the Forties C platform, and now carries around 40% of the UK's oil production. Discovered by BP and lying in Blocks 21/22, the Forties Field is situated almost exactly one degree east of the Greenwich Prime Meridian, which passes through its eastern flank. The £400M forecast to develop this field now looks cheap by comparison, though this was set to more than double by the time it came on stream. The cost of well construction is prominent in any oil company's capital expenditure, and methods are constantly being looked at in working towards reducing these costs.

The Forties main pipeline was laid in 1990 replacing the older, smaller line, and is tied in to the Unity Riser where it passes up and over the platform which stands in 122 metres (400 feet) of water. A riser manifold on the platform enables oil and gas pipelines from more than 25 other offshore fields to tie into either it or the Forties C platform and hence to the main line. All is remotely controlled from the Forties Pipeline Control Centre at BP's Kinneil plant in Grangemouth, which is the operations and communications centre for the Forties Pipeline System, and is manned 24 hours a day throughout the year, with around twelve other oil companies and their partners using the system, not least of which are Shell, Texaco, Elf, and Amerada Hess. The System's capacity is 1,150,000 barrels of liquids and 6,900 tonnes of gas *per day*, and by 1996 more than four *billion* barrels of crude oil had been transported through the pipeline at speeds of up to five kilometres an hour. (Crude Oil was originally stored and sold in wooden barrels, hence the expression).

When in 1973, following the Arab-Israeli 'Yom Kippur' war, a decision was made by Middle Eastern oil producing countries to cut back on oil production and raise the price per barrel to importing countries, the price of UK oil imports spiralled to unprecedented levels, almost trebling in cost over the next year or so. High energy prices result in high inflation, high unemployment, and low growth, and in 1974, along with most of the rest of the industrialised world, the country moved into recession for almost all of the next two years, with unemployment rising to pre-World War II levels, and accruing an extra bill for her oil of nearly £3 billion, emerging only as oil prices stabilised. Just in time, the UK's oil had come on stream in 1975 under the Labour Government of Prime Minister Harold Wilson, when H.M. Queen Elizabeth II visited Dyce near Aberdeen to start the oil off on its journey to the Grangemouth Refinery, five years after the drilling rig Sea Quest first struck oil.

The UK's most northerly field is now 'Magnus' (the Viking Saint of Orkney), discovered in 1974 on acreage licensed to BP, the UK's biggest single producer of oil and gas, on Block 211/12. Whereas a 'giant' platform in the early days of North Sea oil weighed in at around 5,000 tonnes, the 'jacket' (the basic structure at float out) for Magnus weighed a staggering 42,000 tonnes. It stands alone in the Magnus field, the largest fixed platform in steel yet designed and constructed for the North Sea, and has an overall weight of 70,000 tonnes, with a maximum, 'one hundred year' design wave height of 31 metres (100 feet). Its weld material and paint alone weigh almost a thousand tonnes.

Built between 1980 and 1982 by John Brown Offshore at Nigg Bay in the Cromarty Firth, it was in position and producing oil by 1983 from wells drilled to 2,709 metres (8888 feet) below the seabed. It is standing proud in 186 metres (600 feet) of water, and is 312 metres high (over 1000 feet) from the seabed to the top of the flarestack. Lying 160 kilometres (100 miles) north east of Shetland, this field alone was estimated to contain approximately 800 million barrels (a barrel is 160 litres/35 Imperial Gallons) of *recoverable* oil, from a reservoir of more than one and a half billion barrels, formed beneath the ground during the Jurassic period of earth's evolution between 210 and 145 million years ago during the second period of the Mesozoic era when sea levels rose dramatically, and dinosaurs walked the earth.

Current production of 80,000 barrels per day is now carried by a 60 centimetres (24 inch) diameter main export pipeline to the Ninian Central platform where oil is gathered from other fields for its onward journey to the Sullom Voe Terminal in Shetland, one of the largest oil and liquefied gas terminals in Europe. Gas product, along with gas from the Thistle and Murchison fields, is transported ashore using a pipeline shared with Shell/Esso, probably one of the longest in the North Sea, to St. Fergus in Aberdeenshire.

Pipelines such as this are 'pigged' as often as once every two weeks, a system of blowing a large type of bung (a 'pig') through the line to keep it clean, or internally inspect it for corrosion or defects using an 'intelligent' pig which is fitted with sensors or recorders. A pig can also be used to separate different liquids in a line. These lines are also inspected externally on a regular basis either by divers or remotely controlled vehicles.

Built between 1975 and 1981 at a cost of over one billion pounds, and covering around one thousand acres, Sullom Voe terminal provides facilities for a crude oil throughput of around one million barrels per day. Operated by BP it handles production from more than two dozen oilfields, and 26 companies have interests in the terminal, which receives production through the Brent and Ninian pipeline systems. The terminal has sixteen crude oil storage tanks, *eight* of which hold enough oil to supply the UK's total energy requirement for one whole day. In 1998, throughput was around 600,000 barrels a day and tankers shipped oil to refineries all over the world.

Employment associated with the terminal in 1998 was about 500 people. The size and technical complexity of the terminal defies imagination, but it has received the Gold Award for Occupational Safety from the Royal Society for the Prevention of Accidents (RoSPA) over the years.

Though the Magnus output is by no means the largest compared to other fields in the North Sea, its physical size needs to be huge to stand where it is, and does give an idea of what has been accomplished over the intervening years since oil first came on stream, even in those extreme northern latitudes, where the air temperature can be found at around minus 5 degrees C to minus 20 C, and 100 knot winds are not unknown.

By contrast, the most *southerly* oil field in the United Kingdom, also developed by BP, is Wytch Farm, Western Europe's largest *onshore* oilfield in the county of Dorset, and is actually in an Area of Outstanding Natural Beauty, winning in the past the Queen's Award for Environmental Achievement.

People often assume that where there is oil there is bound to be a mess, but this just is not the case. In fact, crude oil and its energy products never see daylight unless you personally spill some petrol (gasoline) as you are hurriedly adding fuel to your car's tank.

Oil is said to have been first observed on a north Mediterranean island hundreds of years BC, but was noted in other places throughout the world too, and was utilised in oil lamps and for medicinal and other purposes, especially to seal hulls of boats and ships. But the very first efforts at drilling the first commercial well were in Pennsylvania, USA, in 1859, when the now well documented Edwin Drake was successful in discovering and recovering vast oil reserves which were found at only twenty metres (65 feet) beneath the ground. Since those small beginnings, world output is now measured annually in thousands of millions of barrels, obtained from every continent of the world except Antarctica, and comes in the shape of more than one hundred different kinds of crude.

Energy and minerals are the life-blood of modern civilisation, and since the Industrial Revolution, Circa 1730-1850, when a mainly agricultural Britain was transformed into one dominated by industry, consumption of them has grown rapidly, and though resources are not unlimited, by the mid-1970's oil and natural gas accounted for nearly 70% of the world's energy production.

These are valuable but non-renewable resources, and derive from organic matter involving both plants and animals, and oil and gas deposits are particularly prevalent in coastal zones. The situations in which they are found are very limited because they can only form under special circumstances.

When marine organisms die they fall and mix with sediments on the sea floor where they gradually become buried under more sediments and dead organisms. These dead phytoplankton and zooplankton form layers thousands of metres thick, and as pressure builds up on the layers the temperature increases proportionally. These organisms are protected from attack by oxidisation, and, mixing with silt and mud, they undergo chemical changes over millions of years that convert the organic material into compounds of hydrogen and carbon, hence 'hydrocarbons', the resulting oil and gas. The oil will mostly move away from its place of formation, as will any gas associated with the oil and, because of their low density, flow upwards through porous sedimentary rocks such as sandstone or limestone. This migration continues until they become trapped beneath a bed of impermeable rock overlying the sedimentary rock.

The commonest form of trap is the anticline where the bed of impermeable rock is folded upwards to form a dome, where the gas accumulates beneath the dome, with the oil immediately below it, where it can be tapped for use. In many cases, the two hydrocarbons are found beneath land in areas where the sea has receded but, as we all now know, in the United Kingdom the majority of oil and gas bearing rocks lie beneath water...in the North Sea.

To be able to locate the possible position of oil and gas deposits beneath the seabed, just as on land, geologists must identify the relevant formations in the rock layers where the hydrocarbons are likely to be trapped, and to do this, various methods of survey are carried out. Methods involved can be by measuring differences in the earth's magnetic or gravitational field, but more commonly by the use of explosive air 'guns' which, in marine seismic operations, send shock waves down through the ocean and deep into the earth's rock strata when the returning waves are picked up by means of a long string of sensitive 'hydrophones' towed behind the vessel creating the shock waves. These hydrophone strings may be two or three kilometres long, and the received sound waves electronically draw a graph on a chart on board the towing vessel, which geologists will analyse and interpret any apparent anomalies in the rock strata indicating that oil or gas may be present. Traditionally, the survey area is shot on pre-determined theoretical lines of position, and the seabed's geographical positions relevant to each shot are accurately recorded by means of localised or worldwide electronic navigation systems, thus allowing prospectors to return to the exact spot they are interested in. Today, of course, positioning will no doubt be by satellite.

From 1970 onwards familiar companies such as BP, Shell, Texaco, Conoco, and Mobil, to name but a few of the major operators, continued to discover, develop, and exploit such important and fruitful fields as those mentioned above, along with fields that today have names that almost all of us are familiar with on a daily basis, such as Piper, Tartan and Claymore, or Cormorant and Thistle to the north. The Forties link-up fields such as Buchan, Britannia, or Montrose, are equally well known, and today there are more than thirty such major companies involved in similar operations in the North Sea, with almost as many contractors represented on many single major installations, either by an individual, or more, or by the presence of its services.

Before the end of that decade, 1978 saw more than half of the United Kingdom's oil requirements being met from North Sea sources, and the future looked exceedingly promising. By 1980, the UK was totally self-sufficient in terms of oil. By then around 100 million tonnes, and around 300,000 jobs with connections to the industry now depended upon it, right down from the man who 'spudded in' the first drill-bit, no doubt ably assisted by essential diver intervention, through the processes of separation, refining, and transportation by pipeline, ship, and ultimately road tanker, to the man who delivers the much needed gasoline or diesel to your local filling station.

According to the latest edition of the government "Brown Book", 'The Development of the Oil and Gas Resources of the United Kingdom 1999', an annual survey of the numbers employed offshore on rigs and platforms was started in 1967, and showed just over 1,000 workers. The number rose steadily through the 1970s to 12,500 in 1978, before falling back in 1979, (although total revenues from oil and gas production in 1978/79 jumped from £574 million, to a massive £2.32 billion in 1979/80).

From 1980 onwards the survey included workers on pipe-laying vessels, crane barges, supply and standby vessels, and in 1991/92 the numbers employed offshore peaked at around 37,000.

These surveys are co-ordinated by the Inland Revenue, with the support of industry provided through UKOOA (UK Offshore Operators' Association), as the main purpose was to assist with tax compliance in the offshore oil and gas industry.

Aggregated results are distributed to government and industry bodies and are used, for example, by the HSE and UKOOA to calculate accident and safety statistics.

Estimates for the 1997 survey gave offshore employment at 23,000, of which 1.5 percent were female, and 93 percent were UK nationals (97 percent from the EU). From the 1999 survey, however, the Inland Revenue estimates that the number employed offshore in 1998 was some 25,500, and the latest figures for 1999 show 27,200.

Not just divers and drillers, roughnecks and roustabouts, of course. We often forget the all-important myriad of other service providers without whom the rigs and installations would find it exceedingly difficult to function - the caterers, cooks and stewards, cleaning staff, and all of the technical service providers such as engineers, electricians, mechanics, welders, riggers, scaffolders and medics, along with a whole host of others, too many to mention, whom we all tend to forget but all of whom are absolutely vital in their own way.

Total revenues shown in the Taxes and Royalties Attributable to UK Oil and Gas Production table (Table 2.5) for 1998/99 were £2.63 billion (down hugely from its 1984/85 peak of £12.171 billion with the collapse of oil prices in 1986), with an additional Gas Levy for 98/99 of £19 million. However, from 1964 to 1999 the overall total contribution to the UK economy, including gas levy, was approximately £95 billion, though recent press reports put the figure nearer to £187 billion. Based on that figure, the average income to the UK over that period was almost £5.5 billion per year, though this pales into insignificance when one considers that, from recent information given by the UK's Automobile Association, the current income to the Exchequer amounts to 75 pence in every pound sterling, (more than US$1.12), spent on fuel. Of total fuel expenditure by the general public over the last twelve months amounting to £24 billion, excluding Value Added Tax at 17.5%, the 'New Labour' Chancellor, Gordon Brown, is sitting very comfortably with his cut. The highest petrol taxes in Europe today, yet we are one of Europe's main producers, and ninth in the world. Latest crude oil production figures for the UK (September 2000) show 2.73 million barrels of oil per day at the current high price of US$33.02 per barrel, though these are volatile times for oil prices as shown at January 2001 when oil is down to $25 a barrel. OPEC is once again considering cutting back on output by 5%, no doubt putting up the price at the pumps again, though a well-known British brokerage firm has recently raised its predicted 2001 average price from $21 to $26 a barrel, arguing that oil stocks are 40% undervalued.

There are sufficient known reserves in the North Sea at the present time for at least another thirty years, and in the world forty years, though the forecast of that number of years seems to remain fairly static as time moves along, as fresh discoveries seem to keep pace with output, and in the UK exploration and the exploitation of new finds moves ever further north and west, and into ever deeper waters. Some sources say that there is much more oil in that sea than has ever yet come out of it. Indeed, BP itself has stated that, "With new discoveries and advances in technology, the North Sea will remain an important oil and gas producing area well into the 21st century."

The high price of oil, and the ever increasing demand for its products, makes the extra effort and cost of deeper water production profitable enough to encourage the major operating companies to keep moving onwards and upwards, and technology is advancing so quickly that it would be virtually impossible to forecast when and where it will all end. In addition, new technology, along with the current high price per barrel, is allowing old wells and the formerly less economic reserves to be exploited profitably, whereas previously they were abandoned, or not commenced, as not worth the required expenditure.

In use since the 1970s, but destined to be used more so in years to come, the greater majority of underwater work in UK waters will probably be done in the deeper waters now being experienced using more advanced Remotely Operated Vehicles (ROV's) to manipulate high tech equipment and tools to support drilling operations, or for construction work or pipeline inspections, or surveys. Remote cameras will, as ever, send pictures back to a topside monitor which are recorded on video-tape for reference, and possibly used by divers utilising one atmosphere diving systems (breathing air within the suit at only atmospheric pressure) to complete underwater works of various kinds at unheard of depths. One company already has viable one atmosphere suits workable to 300 metres (1000 feet) and has developed, and is now manufacturing, a 'Hard Suit' workable to double that depth, with more than a 50-hour endurance capability, and no decompression required.

ROV's are now being joined by the AUV or Autonomous Underwater Vehicle, a small torpedo-like robot which, amongst its many other uses connected with the underwater world, can carry out seabed and pipeline inspections automatically, using satellites for accurate position fixing and control.

Already routine mixed gas diving by diver intervention is possible to over 300 metres, with trials going even deeper, and advanced ROV's have been designed to work in over 2,100 meters (7000 feet) of water for inspection and recovery operations. The new Glomar drillship 'Glomar Jack Ryan' can be fitted out to drill in 3,660 metres (12,000 feet) of water, and major subsea completions are the order of the day, with floating production, storage and offloading units stationed above them. These kinds of systems are utilised for safely and efficiently exploiting deep-water fields, and are also cost-effective in developing marginal fields incapable of effectively supporting the cost of fixed platforms. In 2001 Conoco will probably commence drilling off the Faroe Islands, 320 km north-west of the Shetlands, in 1,000 metres (3,280 feet) of water, and another, the deepest ever in European waters, at an incredible water depth of 1,920 metres (5,883 feet) where, quite clearly, there can be no diver intervention, and the above system in its most highly advanced technical state will no doubt be used if commercially viable quantities of deposits are found.

Though it has been muted by some that one day marine contractors will no longer need to send men beneath the sea, I think that the day when the vital human input of our diving fraternity is no longer needed is a long way off yet. Even should the oil come to an end one day, which no doubt it must, and alternative energy sources be found (though I cannot see at this moment what could possibly replace the many diverse uses of crude oil) someone still has to take it all down again and human diver intervention in the shallower water must certainly be the cheaper option. All speculation, of course, but just one particularly large American offshore construction company has around twenty Dive Support Vessels working at this time, some sixty metres and more in length, spread all around the world, so there's no shortage of diving work to be done.

To-day there are 204 oil and gas fields in the British Sector of the North Sea alone, with many platforms in those fields, all needing close and persistent maintenance to prolong their usefulness, and not least the jobs of thousands of men who continue to go to work aboard them for their just rewards, each making their own contribution, and sacrifice, towards the total effort made in the vastly important task of searching for, finding, evaluating, and extracting our country's very valuable hydrocarbon assets, and transforming those millions of years of evolutionary process into realisable and revolutionary products.

Chapter Three

GETTING IT OUT OF THE GROUND

Scientists can find the conditions that are favourable for the accumulation of oil or gas in a certain area, but the only sure way to know if oil and gas are there is to drill.

Drilling is a very expensive activity with each well costing several million pounds. Even with today's technology, there is still a low probability that oil or gas will be found.

Most oil wells are between 900 and 5,000 metres deep, but it is now possible to drill eight kilometres (5 miles) below the surface, an achievement made possible by skilled operators using powerful equipment and advanced technology. However, the costs of drilling can double or treble when in very deep water, in hostile environments, or when hard rock, high pressure or temperature is encountered. Depending on the texture of the substance being drilled, progress can vary from 50 or 60 metres an hour right down to as little as half a metre in the same amount of time.

To reach the edges of the reservoir, wells are commonly drilled at an angle. It is now possible to drill vertically downwards and then outwards horizontally. This can save a great deal of money as several wells can be drilled from a single point and oil extracted from thin seams of rock.

A BP educational chart 'Oil and Gas from the North Sea' shows that "In the North Sea up to 40 wells may be drilled from the same platform. These may extend up to 5 kilometres (3 miles) from the platform enabling efficient extraction of the oil".

The drill bit, tungsten steel or diamond faced, is turned either with a rotating table on the drill floor, or by a 'downhole' motor attached to a string of steel pipes each approximately nine metres (thirty feet) long, and connected together by hand by highly experienced operators, and the hole is lined with various sizes of steel 'casing' cemented in as depth increases. The derrick, the structure that stands above the hole, must be strong, as the drill bit and pipe are suspended from it. Only a small proportion of the total weight of the drilling string is allowed to bear on the drill bit. This proportion will vary depending on the rock formation being drilled. The derrick must also be tall enough to enable the lengths of drill pipe to be added to or removed from the string.

A drill bit can last from just a few hours to several days, and when a worn drill bit is being changed out for a new one, a 'round-trip', to save on time the drill string is withdrawn from the hole, manually disconnected, stacked inside the gantry, and re-assembled to the new bit three sections at a time, thus the main reason the drill gantry is so high. This operation can today be computerised and carried out automatically, which is vastly more efficient and, importantly, much safer for the operators.

The drilling process is lubricated and cooled by a carefully constituted 'mud', a mixture of clay, water, and various chemicals. The mud passes down inside the pipes to the drill bit and then returns to the top of the hole between the drill string and the sides of the hole, bearing rock debris with it. The mixture is separated with much of the mud recycled, and this provides the geologists with rock samples to indicate the kind of rock the drill is passing through. The weight of the mud also prevents the escape of oil or gas if it is found. If test drilling indicates that oil or gas is present, the drilling of further wells is necessary to determine the area of the reservoir and the amount of hydrocarbons trapped.

Hydrocarbons are classified as solids, liquids, or gases that contain only carbon and hydrogen. Natural gas in its original state is a liquid, but changes to gas under normal pressure at a temperature of around 15 degrees Celsius. Usually the gas or oil is under pressure in the ground, as opposed to what used to be known before the advent of North Sea oil and gas as 'Town Gas', which was made at your local gasworks from coal.

The drilling supervisor can anticipate when drilling is nearing its mark as, in addition to knowing from geological reports at what depth to expect some indication, rock debris will show signs of oil, and temperature at the bit will rise. To stop wasteful and dangerous 'gushers', or 'blow-outs' where exceedingly high pressures can inadvertently be released, heavier mud can be pumped down before drilling is completed, and valves can be closed on blow-out preventers which are fitted to the top of the well casing. A set of valves called a 'Christmas Tree' is fitted to the wellhead to control the flow of gas or fluids from the well.

Discovering new reserves of oil is only the beginning of the story. It's then the job of a new team of economists, scientists and engineers to decide whether - and how - to go into large-scale commercial production.

Once oil and/or gas have been discovered, it has to be established how much is there, how much can be recovered, what its quality is, and how the oil or gas can be transported safely to a refinery or terminal. In other words, is the find economically viable? If so, further wells will have to be drilled and production facilities established.

The fluid extracted from the well usually contains oil, gas and water and it has to be processed so that the crude oil and gas can be transported by pipeline or tanker.

Natural gas is a mix of light hydrocarbons, mainly methane, but also containing ethane, butane and propane. Where there is oil, gas is also found, but gas can form in the presence of little or no oil, hence the large collection of purely gas fields in the southern North Sea.

Crude oil is a natural substance whose composition varies. Even in the same oilfield, where oil is obtained from different depths, it can vary greatly in composition and appearance. It may be an almost colourless liquid or a sluggish, black substance, so heavy that it cannot be pumped at atmospheric temperatures. Generally, however, crude oils look like thin, brown treacle.

The recovery factor, the amount of oil that can be economically extracted compared with the total amount estimated to be in the ground, varies widely. Twenty years ago a recovery factor of about thirty percent was normal. Today the average is about forty-five percent, and improved technology is likely to increase this further.

There is no single solution to getting oil out. Production and transport methods will depend on where the oil is found, and in particular, whether it has been found under the land or under the sea.

Oil is generally found and produced in places far away from where it is used, and a pipeline sometimes hundreds of miles long, or supertanker, or both, may be the only way of getting the oil to the refinery where it will be turned into a usable product.

Since the demise of the coal industry, and people's fear of nuclear energy, we are more reliant than ever on oil, and it affects our lives in many different ways - much more than we realise. A given quantity of crude oil, depending on its quality, produces varying amounts of petrol (gasoline) such as we use in our motorcars, along with other fuels such as diesel, paraffin, aviation spirit, and bottled gas, but an average barrel of oil is said to produce around thirty Imperial gallons of petrol. In addition, naphtha is extracted to be used in the production of many different chemicals and compounds, hundreds of them, not least of which is plastic in all its forms, detergents, disinfectants, paint, adhesives, cling film and even margarine, food preservatives, suntan oil and, especially for the ladies, nail polish. As we approach the end of the Twentieth Century the world is said to be using around 75 million barrels of oil *a day*.

The residue from the distillation of all the various 'fractions' of lighter substances removed and recovered is not wasted, and is used in such common compounds as bitumen and tar for roadworks, roofing materials, and damp proofing in the building industry.

Without all of these things it makes one wonder how the world ever managed before we went beneath the ground and, in the case of the United Kingdom, beneath the sea, and brought the nothing less than miraculous substance of crude oil to the surface, a substance which is the largest source of energy throughout the world. The ingenuity of man to be able to do all of this, and to continue to improve on methods for doing so in such a relatively short space of time in our modern world history, compared to previous generations, is nothing short of miraculous, with man's brilliant technological ability to overcome the adversity of almost any problem laid down before him with breathtaking speed.

Chapter Four

OFFSHORE LIFE (AND DEATH)

I have seen the North Sea and its environs at the height of summer with its surface as shiny smooth as the traditional mill-pond, and with clear blue, cloudless skies, deep translucent and clean cod- filled green water, and a hot sun on my back to match a mood of wonderful well being and thoughts of, "Am I really getting paid for this?"

Winter though is another story, and the general public, because they are not normally involved on a day-to-day basis, have no idea of the horrendous working conditions that can be found in the North Sea. The howling, biting winds, the crash of mountainous seas, the continuous grinding noise on board a drilling rig, the whine of production platforms, or the groan of a pipe-laying barge straining forward on its arm-thick anchor wires, its huge 'stinger' projecting from its rear end, profiled like a gigantic bee sting, and down which the enormous welded pipe is rumbling like thunder as it disappears into the ocean and onto the seabed, for mile upon mile, hardly daring to stop.

Not least of all the continuous cacophony on a platform is the noise from the gas turbines generating all the electricity needed for this city in the sea, not only for its own domestic use but also for the needs of the services required to carry out the tasks of drilling, separating the oil and gas and pumping them ashore, water injection pumps, fire pumps, mud pumps, heating and ventilation, metering, all the various utilities, and the dozens of other essentials, including flaring off gas with its huge flame clawing the night sky sending flickering shadows across the platform decks.

In those winters, often in driving rain or thick fog, all who work there are reminded constantly of the ever present dangers of the hideous possibilities should anything go wrong.

We occasionally hear of, or see on the television news, reports of offshore incidents; a death, a fire, a ditched helicopter or other such like event and, as important as these things are, we still feel somewhat detached from the realities as the news bulletin fades quickly from our minds, and know little or nothing of the daily circumstances surrounding individual mental and physical hardships and dangers faced by all who work there.

One exception to this, of course, was the devastating explosion and fire on the *Piper Alpha* oil platform which was situated approximately 110 miles north-east of Aberdeen, the television pictures of which kept us transfixed as the scenes unfolded before us, and we tried to imagine the horrors experienced by those poor men.

On the evening of 6th July 1988, out of 226 people on board, 165 men lost their lives. Though many divers were onboard, one or two of them actually underwater, mercifully none lost their lives. However, one Diving Consultant, Barry Charles Barber aged 46 of Stranraer, who worked for Aberdeen Offshore Services Ltd, was drowned following the explosion, after apparently successfully leading a party of approximately twenty people to safety. Two Safety Boat crew from a nearby safety vessel who were attempting to rescue survivors also lost their lives, presumably in the huge fireball that came sometime after the initial explosion.

The dreadful conflagration will never be forgotten, and rightly so. More than one hundred recommendations under twenty-four subject headings made in the huge five hundred page report by The Hon. Lord Cullen into the disaster, and presented to Parliament in 1990, caused an astounding amount of improvements to offshore safety.

Health and Safety, and safe working practices have always been of paramount importance throughout the oil and gas industry, both onshore and offshore and, in fact, regulations can be traced back as far as 1934 with the Petroleum (Production) Act, though more appropriate to the offshore industry was the Mineral Workings (Offshore Installations) Act 1971, empowering the Secretary of State to make regulations "for the safety, health and welfare of persons on offshore installations". Other legislation followed, such as the Health and Safety at Work etc. Act 1974, and the Petroleum and Submarine Pipelines Act 1975, under which regulations were made "on a number of subjects including diving operations and inspectors." In 1977 the Health and Safety at Work etc. Act of 1974 was extended to cover workers engaged in the offshore oil and gas industry, including divers, so that the Health and Safety Commission (HSC) "would be responsible for ensuring that common standards of occupational safety were applied both on and offshore".

Acts of Parliaments oblige companies to comply with them, and Regulations made under them, and indeed, most companies voluntarily have their own Health and Safety regimes and publications such as BP's Health, Safety and Environment Journal, *tHe iSsuE* (sic). All companies require safety induction courses and/or briefings of all personnel prior to them going offshore to "maintain the high safety profile" bearing testimony to their commitment.

Offshore workers are constantly aware of the potential dangers surrounding them 24 hours a day and have to live with it and the subconscious realisation, and hidden stress, that there is no getting away from it until the tour offshore is over. Unlike the person who knows the dangers of working in an oil refinery on land, or even a bomb and mine disposal expert who knows that he can almost certainly go home at the end of his working day. Unfortunately, a lot of the safe practises that are now in place are there as a result of past disasters and accidents in which hundreds of offshore workers over the years have been seriously injured or killed. Not only those aboard Piper Alpha and Sea Gem, but in explosions, fires, falls, drilling operations accidents, and from other hazards on the offshore installations, and even helicopter and boat accidents, many of which never come to the attention of the public.

We, the public, hear of major incidents such as the 1965 capsize of the drilling rig *Sea Gem* with the loss of thirteen lives, or the *Piper Alpha* disaster, but we rarely hear other than the vaguest details of those accidents or deaths which happen to one or two individuals such as drillers or divers. The media do not usually report 'in house' enquiries by the companies involved, or investigations by the HSE. Even prosecutions taken by the HSE, the Crown Prosecution Service, or in Scotland the Procurator Fiscal are not widely reported in the press. In the case of a fatality offshore the Coroner, or in Scotland the Sheriff, in whose jurisdiction the incident occurs i.e. Great Yarmouth or Aberdeen, investigates the circumstances, and again the findings are only reported locally. Not, I must say, to keep the matter in any way under wraps because the details are obviously in the public domain, and subsequently a matter of public record, but unfortunately because they are no longer headline news. Once the incident is reported to the appropriate enforcement authority by the installation owner and dealt with, the case is filed and out of the public eye unless it comes to court. In these cases more information comes to light in the public domain but it can be two years or more before the case is heard and for the general public the original incident is practically forgotten, except, of course, for those unfortunates who are related to anyone who has been killed, and have to wait to find out what happened and who, if anyone, was responsible.

In the case of divers, the relevant HSE Offshore Division, Diving Inspection Team, probably in conjunction with the Police, investigate any accident. They will visit the site of the incident; take statements from those persons who were witnesses to the incident, from the deceased diver's employer, usually a diving contractor, and the main contractor. If necessary they will seize equipment and documents and conduct appropriate tests.

The Police and HSE enquiries may initially be carried out from different standpoints. The Police investigation will be directed towards any possible foul play. The HSE specialist diving inspectors will wish to see if any regulations have been infringed. The persons being questioned are likely to be the main contracting company and/or the diving company, to see how they have planned or directed the diving operation; also those persons conducting the dive operation at the dive site, the Diving Superintendent and/or Diving Supervisor. They will of course take note of any possible equipment failure or malfunction.

Prior to the *Piper Alpha* disaster, functions concerned with offshore safety were administered by the Petroleum Engineering Division of the Department of Energy, but the Cullen Report recommended that "these duties should in future be discharged by a discrete division of the HSE which is exclusively devoted to offshore safety and is able to respond promptly and authoritatively to its special needs." Since 1991 the HSE Offshore Division has maintained that responsibility.

Deaths and serious accidents to divers are investigated and reports are made out and acted upon by the appropriate official bodies. HSE inspector's reports may lead to enforcement action including prosecution and/or further advice or guidance, being given to the industry often in a Diving Information Sheet. In some cases consideration is given to amending or consulting on new legal requirements in an attempt to ensure that such accidents can hopefully be avoided in the future.

The most recent innovation under 'The Diving at Work Regulations 1997' is diving sector specific 'Approved Codes of Practice' (ACoPs) which cover not only offshore diving projects but inland/inshore, scientific and archaeological, media and recreational sectors. I would not hesitate to recommend the reading of them to all those involved in such pursuits or pastimes.

Sterling work has been done over many years in connection with Health and Safety in the offshore industry by client companies, contractors, and the regulatory bodies, and this attitude towards such important matters will quite naturally always prevail, as the dangers to such a very vulnerable workforce are obvious and ever present.

Safe working on the factory floor does not stem from something directed by office memorandum, but by individuals developing a deep seated feeling for working safely that at the same time inspires all those he or she comes into contact with to constantly conduct themselves in such manner that everything they do leaves nothing to chance. If the culture is strong at the top, however, which it invariably is, it will permeate down the ladder; the very reason that caring companies are so strong in their approach to all matters of safety and safe working practises.

The value to life and limb of all this may *sound* blindingly obvious, but one does not have to travel too far from these shores to find that little or none of this regulation exists at all. At least it was often the case in the not too distant past, certainly in many countries I have worked in.

But things *are* changing for the better. In most of what are called 'emerging nations' the influence of safety conscious and regulation wise new management teams with experience in the North Sea and other well regulated areas are having an effect. These groups are now easily capable of getting to grips with the provision of safe diving equipment, the recruitment of safe, competent, certificated and experienced professional divers, and overall safe topside and underwater practises.

The lives of a lot of good divers have been lost abroad in the past due to gross incompetence on the part of those responsible for locally run projects, and whom, more often than not, cannot be reached by the ex-patriate's legal representatives, nor indeed be influenced by any unwanted outside interference in their affairs. 'Fair enough' some might say, and they would probably be right to a degree, so it's up to each individual diver to create his own salvation.

The International Marine Contractors' Association has more than 150 companies within its membership. Formed in 1995, its range of company members are spread worldwide, and its interests cover many disciplines including Oil Services, Maritime Services, Consultancies, Engineering, and Marine companies dealing in underwater remote vehicles and diver training, divers, diving, and diving equipment. There is absolutely no reason nowadays why a man looking for diver training or, once trained, for diving work, should concern himself with any company worldwide that is not a member of this esteemed association, which itself has stated that one of the factors attracting new members to the association is the "progressively wider acceptance of the IMCA International Code of Practice for Offshore Diving by clients worldwide."

Chapter Five

THE GOOD OLD BAD OLD DAYS

Unfortunately, as many older divers can vouchsafe, things were not always as safe and well regulated, nor indeed conducted, as they are today, but thank goodness they do necessarily get better with time and the experiences of all concerned, thanks to good, pertinent legislation, good training, and the attainment of very high standards through that training and experience.

Looking back with 20/20 hindsight at things which now make my hair stand on end, amongst some of my own early offshore dives in the North Sea, one was for a commercial diving contractor, using SCUBA (Self-Contained Underwater Breathing Apparatus) on compressed natural air to a depth in excess of 50 metres (165 feet) with no 'buddy', and no attachment to or communication with the surface of any kind, except for a thin, buoyed polypropylene line attached to a pipeline somewhere off in the murky distance, whilst photographing spanning (tidal scouring) beneath the pipeline. Because of that, and a build-up of other such occasions, I took the first opportunity to leave that company to look for another with greater safety awareness.

A diver working for that same, now defunct diving company, and whom I knew well, worked and socialised with, was killed not too long thereafter under circumstances that, to my mind, have never been properly explained.

Many dives were done in SCUBA, off a lifeline, without a lifejacket or reserve air supply, and often without a stand-by diver because, being new to the company perhaps, and because of just the way things were, and needing a job, or wishing to impress, you simply did what you were told almost without question, because if you didn't you could, not could, but would, find yourself out of a job and on the next boat or helicopter back to shore at a single moment's notice. Divers were in short supply, but even so, the toolpushers or barge captains were the bosses and their word was law, and my guess is that nothing much has changed in that respect to this day, except that they are now bound to comply with legal and safe rather than expedient practices.

Some of us knew better, of course, but the facilities, rules and regulations, and even the frame of mind amongst almost everyone in those early days were not there to let you do better. They were pioneering days, and desperate days if, like me, you were out of a job, and would go anywhere and do anything to earn a living and try to get ahead by making a name for yourself in the profession you loved.

Any diver entering the water knows and accepts the risk of how easy it is, if things go wrong, for him to lose his life. Witness divers in my later list who were killed *on the surface*. Not only is he putting his life on the line, but also putting the preservation of that life into the hands of many other people too, some perhaps complete strangers to him, from the top to the bottom of the hierarchy. But, in my experience, it must be said that such an eventuality does not normally even enter a diver's mind, as his training and ability, coupled with a supreme self-confidence, are more than adequate to keep such thoughts at bay.

The diving contractor has the main responsibility, under the Diving Regulations, for ensuring that a safe diving project is carried out. After studying the project and formulating a 'Risk Assessment' he has responsibility for ensuring that all parts of a diving project are managed in such a way as to ensure the safety of all the people involved within it. With further responsibility perhaps is the manager or superintendent who initially organises the project, the engineers who service the diving equipment, the supply boat Captain who transports the equipment safely to its offshore site, the concession owner who also has legal responsibilities. Some or all of these may be unknown to the diver, and yet he must have a blind faith in all of them.

The Diving Supervisor, who will of course be known to the diver, is appointed by the Diving Contractor, and on being appointed he has a duty to direct any diving job safely, and sets up the job on site and gives the word to go. His word is law, and if he considers that any aspect of the job is unsafe he must not proceed, and report the fact to the contractor.

Not least of all is the diver's tender, who dresses him and checks all his equipment, right down to the last safety connection or pin, and that everything connected with the divers' apparel is sound and in place. After that it is the diving supervisor and his topside crew who have the onerous duty of ensuring a safe and effective dive whilst complying with all legal regulations, and management provided diving rules, right down to the last letter of the law because, should he be found negligent in any way in the event of a fatality or serious injury he will most certainly be held to account, and in the event of a fatality could very well face a charge of manslaughter, and if found guilty go to prison, as has happened in the past.

Dive Control Panel

It is also incumbent upon the management of the offshore installation to provide safe working conditions, and to provide the Diving Supervisor with sound weather information for the area in which the diving is being carried out for the complete duration of that diving operation. This is always monitored on the platforms on a day-to-day basis anyway as to sea state and general meteorological conditions, and especially on drill rigs where these reports could be critical.

Surface orientated diving means that the diver will enter the water from the surface and return back to the surface on completion of a dive. The dive supervisor cannot personally check every single detail of a dive, especially when he's mostly inside running the dive station, and responsible delegation must be inherent in any dive procedure. This is where a most serious responsibility falls upon the last delegated man in the line, the man holding onto the other end of the diver's umbilical. When surface orientated diving is taking place he must make sure that he is not holding the diver too tightly, nor 'tending the tide' in letting out too much of the umbilical. It is *very* easy to let out too much, pulled by the tide or current, the bight of the umbilical therefore being able to get snagged up somewhere, or into anchor hawser guide wheels such as on an anchored semi-submersible rig; pipe rolling down a stinger on a pipe-laying barge, or even into a boat's dynamically positioned or other vessel's propellers or thrusters.

A semi-submersible is self descriptive, where, for simplicity, the drill rig sits on a platform which in turn sits on huge tanks or pontoons anchored to the seabed, or held in place by Dynamic Positioning, as with the later mentioned pipe-laying barges, that can be flooded part way down to float like an iceberg and make the platform more stable with the weight of water inside; very necessary in rough seas. This of course will put anchor wire guide sheaves beneath the water's surface and a potential hazard to divers is therefore created as the wires move up and down and the sheaves seesaw with the movement of the ocean. Many such rigs now have a Dynamic Positioning capability, but that in itself has created its own special hazard for diver's 'umbilicals' should the system go down, as will later be seen.

I have personally been involved in such a heart-stopping occasion involving a poorly tended umbilical when, in the Middle East, a diver was at about thirty metres (100 feet), on natural air, and was being tended by a young, inexperienced diver over the stern of a small diving support vessel which was attached, stern to, to a seabed anchorage point for one of the chains of a Single Buoy Mooring or SBM (an offshore oil loading buoy) by a wire hawser - an open water operation carried out successfully many, many times before.

The tide had started to run and the dive was aborted. The tender had thought that the pull on the hose was the diver moving about on the bottom, when all the time the tide had been taking the umbilical under the stern of the boat, inexorably into the support vessels stopped propeller. When the diver came to release the wire from the anchorage point, the order was given to the dive deck by the man on the inboard end of the diver's radio, for the tender to take up the diver's slack. (An instruction *always* given when a diver is about to leave the bottom).

The tender took up the slack, feeling what he thought was the diver at the other end, but what he was actually feeling was the vessel's propeller. When the vessel's skipper was given the order to give the propeller a quick burst astern, to move the vessel backwards to allow the diver some slack to release the downwire and then drift off the anchorage point with it before ascending the wire, the umbilical was immediately drawn into the propeller.

All communication was lost as 30 meters of umbilical was ripped off the vessel's deck, and then what seemed like an eternity of horror-filled time, as the stand-by diver was hurriedly prepared. Suddenly the diver was on the surface, trailing not many remaining metres of umbilical, and all hell was let loose to get him on board and recompressed in the deck chamber.

Fortunately the umbilical had severed before the diver was drawn into the propeller and, after a spell on oxygen in the chamber, he emerged "shaken but (apparently) not stirred". If he's reading this today, he knows he's a very lucky man, and no doubt the tender learned a lifelong lesson.

The remains of the total of 100 metres (300 feet) of umbilical when recovered from the propeller were an inextricable bundle approximately two metres long by about half a meter across. A salutary lesson for all concerned.

A diver lost his life in the North Sea in 1976 when diving from the Construction/Pipelaying Barge 'Orca' (later described), when too much of his umbilical was let out in a tideway and had got snagged up somewhere. The stand-by diver could not recover him until the tide eased some hours later, when the diver was found drowned. This man worked for me in the Middle East and was a good, safe diver, so it just goes to show what can happen even when everything seems to have been in order, and all rules complied with.

Another diver, just 29 years old, also lost his life in the North Sea when his umbilical, and subsequently he himself, was drawn into the blades of a thruster (later described) on the 'Stena Orelia' in 1995. So it will be seen that the job of tending a diver's umbilical while he is in the water is not one on which a man can afford to be less than seriously attentive, even if the diver is only a couple of metres down.

I am not suggesting for one moment that this was the case in the first of the two fatalities above, but negligence was certainly found in the second, and they are classic examples of what can happen to the unwary. It's not uncommon for a diver to get snagged up underwater, especially in conditions of poor visibility, but happily on most occasions he is able to resolve the situation for himself or, if not, the problem can probably be quickly sorted by the stand-by diver. But not always, as we will see!

Even though, quite naturally, the technology of diving and its accompanying systems has vastly improved over the last thirty-five years, and many new safety initiatives have been put into place, and have undoubtedly been effective, these things still happen occasionally, surprisingly often in the shallower water depths rather than the deep sea gas diving underwater world which one might consider to be the more dangerous of the two. But then of course, in the deeper water, the diver is not so far from his tender, and the bell is his safe haven, but even then snarl ups have occurred, and more than one of those has resulted in a diver losing his life.

Returning to those early days it was a matter of 'have flippers, will travel', and though I was an experienced ex-navy diver, (which *didn't* make me an oilfield diver by any stretch of the imagination), good judgement was clouded by other considerations. Like paying bills and feeding your family for a start, and almost anyone, with very little experience, could get diving work in the North Sea, and stood themselves, unknowingly but willingly, into danger.

There was good money to be made, this was the new Klondike, and if there was any chance at all, we were going to be a part of it. And there were chances. There was an obvious shortage of divers experienced in oilfield work, and we were given the jobs and the chance to learn. It was the gold rush all over again, and anyone with a fighting chance was not going to be left out.

Many of those divers have been described by some in the past as "Cowboys", or accused of having forged diving certificates, but mostly by people not associated with, and dependent on, those who were waiting outside the factory gate, so to speak, experiencing the need to find themselves a job at that time. If that's being a cowboy, then so be it. Besides, without wishing to seem supercilious, I recently read in a newspaper somewhere that, "The term cowboy was first applied during the American Revolution to bands of marauders organised by, and loyal to, the British Imperial cause." I guess that just about sums it up! Except that this cause was their very own, and rather an urgent one!

And what of the diving contractors and installation owners? They employed the divers after all, so there was just as much need and urgency on the part of the employers to get the work done as there was on the part of the divers to get the work, so it is totally unfair to direct the responsibility for so many diver deaths on the divers themselves. After all, safety legislation has existed in some form or other almost since the Industrial Revolution itself, and it was incumbent upon employers to ensure the suitability and safety of their workers even then.

It has also been said that a lot of the 'divers' were not divers at all, but just *said* they were, having picked up a few tips from their mates. I can hardly believe that this is true, and most definitely was not in my experience. In the North Sea I never met a diver who could not put in a decent days work underwater, or who wasn't a diver of some kind or other, or who ever forged a diving certificate. I'm not saying it didn't happen, only that I never came across nor heard of any such thing. In fact, in 23 active years in diving, I only ever came across three divers whom I thought were incompetent, and only one of those was a "Brit", and none of them were in the UK. It would be naïve of me to think that, even today, diver's certificates are not stolen or misappropriated; they are a valuable item, and they can get lost, so it's up to the individual, and I'm sure it is the case, that he fully realises that his diver qualification certificate is his livelihood.

Yes, we were inexperienced *oilfield* divers, but in the UK at that time there *were* no British oilfield divers, nor oilfield training to be had, as schools for gaining that type of training just did not exist here in the very early days, because there was no expectation of need. Yes, with the exception of ex-service divers, they had no Part this or Part that diving certificates, but that follows the 'no training to be had' theme mentioned above, and a lot of them were pure amateurs, or "Scooby Doos" as even we ex-RN divers playfully called them. Where would they get professional training and a certificate? Very expensively in America, perhaps, because the oilfields were there, and good training was to be had there; though not through government organised and approved schemes, and who could afford it? Sure, we played a lot of catch up, but it just all seemed so natural at the time, and if one looks at the statistics of diving accidents *after* the 1974 Safety Regulations came into force it will be seen that the incidence of fatalities *increased* in the early years thereafter, though it was certainly before they had time to bite.

Yes again, prospective divers had no medical certificates to say they were fit to dive, though they had a certificate from their doctor saying they were fit and healthy. (There was no such thing as an "approved doctor".) What more could a diving company ask for? There was no such thing as a certificate to say you were fit to dive offshore in the North Sea either, or anywhere else offshore in the UK for that matter. There were no relevant offshore Regulations either around the first or second year of the 1970s, until probably the Mineral Workings (Offshore Installations) Act 1971, so who was to be guided where to do what by whom in what kind of way?

There is no doubt that this lack of oilfield experience may have been responsible in part for some deaths and accidents, but few and far between in my opinion, and as I've said elsewhere in this book, many more drillers and the like were killed also, so what does that mean? Even in the years 1979 to 1989 when everything was so well regulated and well thought out, with massive safety regulations and practises in place, there were 16 "drilling" deaths compared to 6 divers. I realise that there were many more of the former in the field of offshore employment than there were of the latter, but the fatalities still occurred.

Personally, I'm glad that things were frontier-like in the very beginning, otherwise many of us would never have got a start in the oilfields in the first place, and that takes in a good 90% of those men who did it as they went along, learned as they went along, got qualifications as the opportunities presented themselves, and turned out to be excellent divers, supervisors and, yes, even managers. The fact that safety considerations were lacking or lagging behind was no fault of the divers, and were they to wait until completely wrapped in cotton wool, and all the jobs were gone? Of course not!

Safety Regulations came along eventually and were welcomed by all concerned, and there is no doubt whatsoever that fatalities and accidents were prevented because of them, and all credit to the diving inspectorate who were instrumental in getting those regulations implemented.

I started off in the oilfields as a lowly ex-RN Leading Seaman diver because, although I enjoyed my service time, money-wise I couldn't wait to get out of the Navy where I had been earning £7 for a 24-hour day, seven-day week. Following my demob' I slowly became a good civil engineering diver, and later a good salvage diver, and later still, a damn good oil-field diver, learning it all as I went along.

And though I'm obliged to say it myself, I later became a good Supervisor too, supervising during one particular two year period the Increased Capability Diving Task Unit of a diving company which was on contract to the biggest oil company in the Middle East, and even as a diver was personally instrumental in the completion of three of the then world's largest underwater oil related installations. We were a mobile diving unit in the Arabian Gulf capable of any kind of air diving operation, including burning, welding, and underwater television film making on many kinds of inspection, construction, and maintenance and repair tasks to which we were assigned as a working unit.

For my sins I was later appointed Diving Manager within the same company, by highly respected and experienced American higher diving management, when I surpassed existing and long serving diving supervisors within the same company. Hence the old adage about little acorns, perhaps? I am a firm believer that a man who has come up through the ranks has considerably more to offer than the average university graduate turned diving manager, and top slots are not occupied by *incompetent* tired old divers despite what has been said on the subject to the contrary. There is no substitute for good experience gained over many years.

I feel I have needed to go on at some length about this as many of those early divers did just as well, if not better, getting good qualifications and earning good money as the opportunities presented themselves, and ended up working in positions of responsibility for quality international diving companies, some even having their own companies, both at home and abroad. But in many cases of diver death, these often fell victim to circumstances that had not, and could not, have been foreseen, and that were most certainly very often beyond their immediate control. Despite high levels of safety awareness, offshore diving companies and main contractors were, and still are, being prosecuted and convicted for criminal acts or omissions, though no one these days, most certainly, would commit any *deliberate* act in the knowledge that someone might be killed or injured because of that act or omission. Unlike the risks that *were* taken, and potential hazards that *were* ignored by employers in the past for the sake of expediency.

It's said that accidents don't just happen, but I think in ever changing circumstances they do, and it's up to all of us to learn, as we most certainly do, from those circumstances, and to make sure that it, or something like it, doesn't happen again.

Some reports of diver fatalities that I have seen, and have copies of, are exceedingly ambiguous in statements such as "it is thought the diver did this" or "it is assumed the diver did that", or " it is not known…" It will never be known what the actual causes leading to many diver fatalities were, nor what thoughts or feelings the divers had in those last moments of life. It certainly wasn't, "this is happening to me because I'm not really a qualified diver", and I abhor any suggestion that this may have been the case. I most certainly will never believe that as many of them died by their own acts or omissions as seems to have been indicated, though in conversations with knowledgeable people closely involved I have to admit that they have sometimes put up a good argument.

These men were the salt of the earth and prepared to work long and hard in conditions that they had no reason to believe would cost them their lives, in an effort to make something out of those lives. In those days it was all push to get the oil out, and the 'toolpushers' (and diver pushers) were God, and had to be obeyed.

All offshore operations are that much safer today, of course, particularly since specialists in the various offshore professions were appointed in drilling, engineering and not least in diving, and with the later introduction of offshore diving regulations covering amongst many other pertinent rules and regulations; working conditions, medical examinations, diver certification, provision of certain types of equipment, testing of equipment, record keeping, and responsibilities of installation owners, diving contractors and diving supervisors. And there is, too, the Diving Inspectorate to keep everyone on their toes.

The Offshore Installations (Diving Operations) Regulations 1974, (see page 184), were made and laid before Parliament in July 1974, and came into effect on the 1st January 1975, though six divers affected by those Regulations died in that same year; four in the British Sector of the North Sea, and two in British Territorial

Waters at Scapa Flow. In addition, in 1976, seven divers died in the British Sector of the North Sea, plus one in Loch Fyne, and one in Anglesey.

1977 saw a vast improvement, if one can call it that, when three divers died in the British Sector, and two divers lost their lives in the same incident on Beryl A platform in 1978 in 117 metres (380 feet) of water when the 'bell' (later explained) became detached from the lifting wire, and a further three in the British Sector in 1979, one where the diver's helmet came off, and a further two when, once again, the bell wire became detached from the bell, (all later described). Did these men die from their own incompetence? Certainly not!

But there were no deaths then until 1982, proof positive that by that time the various Regulations were making a definite contribution towards improving overall safety, and vast amounts of experience were being gained also which, it is agreed, in its own way, was as instrumental in preventing diver deaths and accidents as the regulations were themselves.

The most satisfying leap was from August 1984, to July 1995, when no deaths of divers whatever were recorded in the British Sector of the North Sea, though a British diver was drowned in the Norwegian Sector in 1987. The penultimate diver of the Century lost his life in 1996 through negligence on the part of his employers, and the last in 1999 through an underwater explosion when using burning gear, following which an Aberdeen based sub-sea engineering company admitted a breach of health and safety regulations resulting in the fatality.

Chapter Six

THE RIGHT STUFF

The extraction of oil and gas is not and never was some kind of heroic, reckless adventure in which we all play or played our best part. Over the years men went seriously to work, not to war, to earn an exceedingly good living for themselves and their wives, loved ones and families, but a lot of whom died carrying out their normal day's work. These were men of various professions; roustabouts and riggers, engineers and drillers, deckhands and the divers too, and it is the latter, of course, some of whom I knew and worked with, and who died horribly and mostly alone, to whom, as I have said, I hope to be able to pay a well deserved and enduring tribute.

Diving in its purest sense is only a method of transport, a means of getting to work, the person fit and able to carry out a day's skilled work when arriving on site. But the diver also needs a system able to support and maintain him there for the dive duration and, like any 'normal' professional, he needs to get to work in good health, in good heart, and with the undoubted capability of being able to accomplish a given task in the best possible way and in the best possible time. However, in my opinion, no further comparison can be made between what we might call a 'normal', worker and a professional commercial diver, and least of all our modern day oilfield diver with his need of a range of mental skills, and a definite physical aptitude in the use of technologically improved tools, that compares exceedingly favourably with the highest trained of artisan in any profession in the land, but which must necessarily be put to use under the most arduous and unnatural of working conditions.

This particular diver, so often an extrovert of the highest order, first needs to be mentally, though not necessarily physically strong. He needs, and does have, courage in abundance, and an overpowering determination to complete his part of the task, not least in the face of criticism from his own work colleagues. This diver is the best at what he does, especially when ashore with a few pints inside him, tending to enliven the stories. But in most cases, I would not argue that what he says is untrue!

Most divers, when fully trained and with a few years of experience, are accomplished seamen and riggers, welders and burners, and not without a fair modicum of mechanical and electrical knowledge; and some are qualified medics. All divers engaged in commercial activities, on as well as offshore, must possess a valid and in date First Aid at Work certificate. There are very few, non-medical professions in the world that I know of that demand that additional skill, though all Offshore workers in the UK require basic First Aid knowledge. In addition, divers need to be competent in blueprint interpretation, the tools of underwater television production, still photography, non-destructive methods of testing for corrosion on underwater structures, epoxy applications, grouting, hydro and sand blasting, ship hull inspections and repair, salvage operations, paint applications, water-jetting, building and demolishing, the use of explosives, and methods of knowledgeable inspections of all kinds, and especially of oilfield hardware, with the ability to give a true, lucid, and comprehensive report on all or any of those, often under exceedingly arduous conditions, in poor or nil visibility, on the nature of the job at hand.

Some people might find just some of that difficult sitting behind a desk in a comfortable warm office on dry land. Try it 150 meters underwater in the middle of the night, in gloomy and icy cold conditions whilst often trying to concentrate on the simple act of breathing, being constantly aware of the unnaturalness of one's shadowy surroundings, and the turgid movement of a huge body of water, whilst trying, sometimes with difficulty, to make oneself heard and understood.

Communications are exceedingly important at any time and without them the dive should be aborted, as it is actually illegal for a diver to even go into the water, let alone remain underwater, without them. In addition, communications should be recorded and the recordings kept for at least 48 hours after a particular dive is completed.

There is an accepted responsibility on the part of any diver not only to take an interest in, but also to fully understand the diving systems, and the equipment that he wears to get him to his place of work, and the systems that operate to sustain him whilst he's there. He will also be fully conversant with ever more technical tools and equipment, so that when he gets to his place of work, deep under the sea, often in darkness, he will more readily be able to coordinate his thoughts and physical capabilities to carry out his task in the efficient manner required of him by his topside masters, often under what must surely be the world's most trying and arduous working conditions.

Commercial diving tasks are many and varied, and rapid technological change has accentuated the use of many new types of diving equipment, gas mixes, and approaches to the art of diving over the last ten to twenty years, but on a day to day basis tasks generally fall within three main categories - construction, inspection, and maintenance, and an oilfield diver can be employed on any, or indeed all of these categories in a single day, using various types of equipment, and this would not be unusual in areas of relatively shallow water such as the Persian Gulf (Arabian Sea).

He must be supremely fit, and fearless in where he goes in the underwater world, and though generally at ease with his diving situation, he must never forget that he is out of his natural environment and sensibly - not without *some* apprehension, because that's what keeps him alive - be alert to any possible danger. It's said that if you ever meet a diver who says he's never been scared underwater, he's either a liar, or a nutcase.

He therefore, metaphorically speaking, and quite subconsciously, keeps one hand for the Navy and one for himself as we used to say, often in dark and icy cold conditions, and sometimes fast running water where it's not unknown to have gloves ripped off, and hands torn just trying to hold on to the job. This is perhaps not a common event, but is certainly not unknown, though diving supervisors generally attempt to avoid continuing diving operations once the tidal current picks up. But a heavy build-up of water can occur very quickly during a dive, making conditions extremely hazardous, especially if a job is of greater than normal urgency, and there is a panic on to get it completed in a hurry.

So here we have a rather unique man in many ways and, without doubt, a man doing what can be, in certain circumstances, one of the most dangerous, and certainly the most lonely and sometimes frightening jobs in the world. I say *one* of the most dangerous jobs, because statistics bear out the fact that more deaths and serious injuries occur during offshore drilling operations than diving operations, though it would be an interesting statistical exercise to explore the percentages of deaths and accidents over the years amongst the various crews, compared to actual numbers employed offshore in their respective professions.

In 1997 for instance, diving personnel represented only 0.9 percent of the total of an estimated 23,000 offshore workers, whereas in drilling operations the numbers employed represented 16.4 percent of the workforce.

Divers will be the last to admit to anyone that diving is dangerous, playing down the dangers by stating, and rightly so, that diving is made especially safe today with new regulations, more modern equipment, and certainly more professional and well-trained supervisors and divers. However, something serious can happen to a person employed on land in the ordinary course of daily life and assistance of all kinds is immediately available to him or her. But diving and its circumstances are *extraordinary*, and when a diver is hanging like a pendulum weight on the end of his umbilical a couple of hundred meters underwater, and something goes seriously wrong, as it does from time to time, there is often no professional help immediately to hand, and sometimes no way back, even though every effort is made to help his situation.

Yes, divers are loud, and they brag, and they get drunk, and they fight, and they bull a lot, and they laugh a lot, and they try to be one of the crowd, but deep inside they are mostly solitary individuals, and many of them often actually enjoy and prefer their own company. This stems, as is obvious, from the fact that their working life has a lot to do with self preservation in a lonely underwater world where, even though there is someone on the end of the 'phone, they may just as well be a million miles away.

One overcast winter's day in Japan, on 'Rest and Recuperation' from Korean coastal patrols, I watched our ship's divers trying to recover a valuable piece of anchor chain that had been lost overboard in Sasebo harbour from our own ship, HMS Birmingham. I knew them all well and, over time, noted that though they worked well as a team when diving, they all seemed to be extraordinarily single-minded and strong willed individuals in their private lives and, though they were Navy men, each was seemingly in pursuit of his own individual goals.

Being a bit of a solitary sort of person myself, and relishing time spent alone, it came to mind that this could be the kind of job for me. Even as a young sailor I often went ashore on my own and not along with the crowd. I was 17 years old at the time, and by the age of 19 I had realised my ambition after spending 15 weeks getting a close up view of the bottom of Chatham Dockyard, in Kent, and then went home to Mum with a nice shiny gold-wire diver's helmet badge sewn to the cuff of my uniform. The course was in two parts, and after the first three weeks, if you passed, the badge was a diving helmet with SW underneath for Shallow Water diver, but the big boys couldn't resist every opportunity to take the rise and called us Shark Wrestlers. After that it was all *uphill,* but if you made it to the top you were well on the way.

I have loved every moment of the diver's life from the very first day, and though I have spent days and nights frozen half to death, covered in oil, inside as well as outside of a wetsuit, for best part of a week on a grounded tanker; dragging out dead bodies; being underneath grounded ships in the pitch black dark with screeching, grinding steel all around you; breaking ice on winter days to get into the water; and tossing about on storm driven dark oceans with half of it *inside* the boat, I have never regretted my decision to enter the profession for one single moment, even though in the first few weeks of my Navy diver training I did wonder about my apparent foolhardiness.

Of course there have been good times too, lots of them, when I have almost had to pinch myself in total disbelief that someone would actually pay me to do what I was doing. Overall though, the dirty dark dives have outnumbered the pretty coloured fish dives, so don't believe everything you see on the television. But even so, like every other diver I have ever met, there has never been one single day of regret that I queued up at those early factory gates of diving opportunity.

Chapter Seven

IT HAS TO BE THE MONEY

It is a most peculiar fact of Murphy's Law that there is no oil to be had in the Bahamas or the Seychelles, or other suchlike places, to make the oilman's lot a very much happier one. Living and working offshore in some of the world's most stinking hot, dirty, or freezing cold and remotest areas is totally representative of the usual locations and conditions that the marine oilman finds himself in. And for that matter, most of those who work on land, too. But, as far as I am aware, oil has never yet been found in anyone's backyard (except by the Beverly Hillbillies, for those who remember them on TV), so those who seek the black gold are obliged to go wherever it *is* to be found.

The North Sea is probably one of the worst in the world, save perhaps Alaska, for working conditions during six long winter months, but is well compensated with good wages, good food and comfortable, sometimes almost luxurious accommodation, endeavouring to make up for all the other things that workers might consider are missing from their isolated existence.

Known to the layman as 'the rigs', there are very many different kinds of offshore platform, hundreds of them in the North Sea, both permanent and temporary. Some are drill rigs of various types; semi submersibles, and 'jack-ups', and many are production platforms where, after all drilling work is completed, a 'jacket' specially constructed for that site is set in position over the well or wells drilled. Some are pumping stations, receiving oil from surrounding platforms, and some are used for oil storage, or accommodation purposes whilst a platform is being worked over for whatever reason, and some are completely unmanned, being operated remotely. Many installations are completed sub-sea and are also, obviously, remotely operated and thus are never seen except by divers or ROV's.

No matter what or where though, where men are at work, working conditions are ultra-safe, as they should be everywhere, and all personnel of every persuasion are issued with their own personal protective clothing and equipment which must be worn at all times when stepping outside, unless diving, of course. Survival suits and life jackets are issued and worn for helicopter flights out to the platforms, and there are strict rules for getting on and off these flying workhorses that must be learned and obeyed to the letter. On arrival at a platform you can hand your lifejacket to someone taking an inbound flight, but retain your survival suit for your return journey, and in case you need it aboard, though there are plenty of those on every platform. Basic First Aid, Fire-fighting and Sea Survival skills are all necessary pre-requisites for anyone wishing to work offshore, although these latter qualifications can all be combined in one course, and such courses are readily obtainable, at your own cost. Addresses of schools approved for this training are available from diver training centres. All of this is applicable to all no matter what your profession or skill. It applies to drillers and divers, cooks and stewards, roustabouts and roughnecks, and even the platform manager. No one is excused. A far cry from those early days of 'have flippers, will travel'.

Reporting to the admin' office on arrival you will be briefed as to your accommodation and your emergency station, and given details of do's and don'ts, who your safety rep' is, and the location of your muster point for gathering in the event of an emergency. Drills are held from time to time, sometimes at unearthly hours, to make sure that everyone knows where they should be in case of such emergency, and exactly what they are required to do. Basically, it's the same as getting aboard any merchant ship (or warship come to that)...everyone is required to know where their lifeboat station is, and how to conduct themselves safely in the interim.

There is a vast difference between the facilities available to workers on a large fixed platform compared to those on smaller units, basically because the fixed platform is permanent, as its name implies, and has far more available leisure space for the likes of a laundry, cinema, library, gymnasium etc. Some even have a sauna and other leisure activities such as satellite television, whereas units such as pipe-laying and derrick barges do not have that luxury of space, to allow the full scope of such amenities, and of course they are constantly on the move.

However, once a man is able to work, weather permitting, he pays no real thought to where he is, and could be on any one of a hundred locations throughout the world - the work being so very similar in nature. In fact in some work locations the day of the week is not only unknown to the individual but, more often than not, is totally irrelevant anyway.

On many small units, and in many foreign locations, there is often no knowledge of Monday to Sunday, there being no weekends off, and sometimes no night and day depending on what job you do, only perhaps the odd bit of time off when working relatively close to shore. Even then there is often nowhere to go, and sometimes the itinerant native entrepreneur selling beer from an icebox on the beach is the only distraction. Often abroad a man can work for six months without a break, seven days a week, or even a year or more at a time, with supplies and mail brought out by boat, with not a helicopter in sight. The men who put up with these conditions, in general, are there for no other reason than the money, no matter what anyone else might tell you.

Most offshore workers do like their jobs. It's just that often, in those kinds of circumstances, they would rather be doing it somewhere else.

On many small working 'platforms', including the construction and pipe-laying barges mentioned, accommodation is sparse, though reasonably comfortable. Divers are normally four, or even eight, to a cabin or 'Portakabin' in which there is little room to do anything but sleep, and that is often disturbed by the comings and goings of different shifts, or a diver getting up for his turn to 'get wet'. Work is often around the clock, weather permitting, and food is almost continuously on the go. This can be indifferent to excellent, and where it is the latter, you sometimes need a separate plate for the chips.

A fixed platform complex, depending on size, could have anywhere between eighty and two hundred or so men on board, a lot of them on twelve hour shifts and having completed a shift, and after a good meal, the average offshore worker will be found catching up on his sleep. There are, though, films and videos, books to read from the onboard library, cards, chess and darts to pass any waking time, dependent on location and type of work unit.

Some very small construction or pipe-laying barges, certainly in my experience, can be miserable billets. These are mostly abroad from the UK, with poor accommodation, often not very clean, poorly produced food, little or no hot water, sparse mail, news or newspapers, and films non-existent, with little or nothing to do outside of your daily work schedule. Eating or sleeping gets you away from the mind numbing boredom between dives, or perhaps a spot of fishing if someone has been forward thinking enough to bring out some tackle. At night I have seen spears made up from broom handles with sharpened welding rods attached at one end, and a piece of rope as a lanyard at the other, with people spending hours on end attempting to spear the multitude of sea snakes swimming on or near the water surface attracted by the bright deck lights.

Downtime for bad weather can be absolutely horrendously boring, with days at a time when nothing can be done, and the sea is a foaming mess of green, white-capped water. Most divers will exercise though, and if there is no equipment they often make their own. Dumbbells and barbells can be made up out of scrap iron as there's usually plenty scattered around, or they will do pull-ups on various convenient cross-braces, or sit-ups and press-ups. Most divers I have come across have taken an interest in keeping fit, and if near a piece of easily accessible land will walk, run, or have a game of football to keep off the pounds the food will surely put on if you're not careful.

In years past alcohol on board was always banned, and was a sacking offence if found in your possession, though I believe a more liberal attitude is taken in certain circumstances these days with rationed allowances in some civilised though remote areas. Our survey boat Captain once magically produced four bottles of Jack Daniels bourbon on one Brazilian offshore Christmas Day! As far as I am aware though, along with many other items that could cause a problem, it is still banned in the North Sea. The list is extensive, but logical when we are talking of things such as cigarette lighters and matches. Smoking is prohibited on many platforms, even in your own cabin, though on most platforms there are certain areas set aside for such activities, governed by strict rules.

Offshore workers, especially divers, should never be envied their salaries or home lifestyles, because without any doubt whatever they have earned every penny the hard way, often under the most unenviable of working conditions.

Take for example those divers who worked on the salvage of 5½ tons of gold from the British heavy cruiser HMS Edinburgh which, during World War 2, was under the command of Captain Hugh Faulkner, RN, and while returning to the UK with Russian gold destined for the US in exchange for war supplies, was sunk in the Barents Sea. Many years later, although some divers were changed out, others spent around forty days locked inside a steel chamber complex, going down to a seabed war grave in a diving bell to recover over £40 million (sterling) of gold from a highly dangerous, oily bomb room, full of overhanging ordnance and huge pieces of jagged steel. They flame cut their way through that steel in the presence of bombs, ammunition, and skeletons of long dead sailors - part of the crew of 57 officers and men killed on the day of the sinking, in a world record depth for diver intervention salvage work in around 245 metres (*800 feet)* of icy black water, with the diving vessel way above them, held in position only by a very fallible dynamic positioning system.

They made millions for the salvage company, the diving company bosses, the Russian Government, and the British Government, and lots of money for other people too, and they themselves got far and away less than anyone else involved for a job which, without a doubt, could not have been done without them! Now you may think that whatever they earned on a job like that, even though it was taxed, it must have been a considerable amount of money for five to six week's work, but believe me when I tell you that it was a lot less than some people earn in a week for kicking a football around. So stop and think about it, read it again perhaps, and you may soon be of the mind that *you* wouldn't do it in those conditions for twice as much of whatever it was, and perhaps not even at all! Oh! There's something I forgot to mention. If they hadn't found the gold and recovered it, they wouldn't have got a payday. It was, 'No cure, no pay' to quote that famous salvage business expression.

During the offshore worker's fourteen or twenty eight day work cycle, he often thinks on a daily basis of the simple things he's missing, but which most people in other home based professions take totally for granted - a stable home life for instance. He's sometimes told he's lucky when seen with his new car, or sitting in the garden of his brand new home. If being lucky is endangering the loss of those things, along with his marriage due to enforced absences, being unable to help in bringing up the kids, or be there for their birthdays, or even Christmas, (work goes on in the oil production business 365 days a year), or just go down to the pub, take the dog for a walk, indulge in his normal sports or hobbies, or sleep in his own blissfully quiet and stable bed, then he doesn't need any bad luck, as he gets none of those things on an everyday working basis. What many divers do get is a lot of home strife, broken marriages and divorce - it seems to go with the territory.

I remember reading somewhere once about a famous American dramatist who had four plays running on Broadway at the same time. His mother was congratulated by a neighbour saying how lucky he was. "Yes", she said, "and the funny thing is, the harder he works, the luckier he gets."

Luck has nothing to do with anything in the final analysis. It's his chosen profession in which he works damn hard, and for which he has made sacrifices to get himself well qualified, and so he commands good money, for which he is prepared to make further sacrifices, and he gets on with the job with a will and to the very best of his ability, but though he knows he may well miss it, he still looks forward to the day when he will be able to give it all up and live a very normal life again.

As with military service, the stresses and strains on a man are ever present, often exacerbated by his own self if, perhaps, he is working on a four weeks on, four weeks off system, which is common enough, and he then goes home and tries to change the world - the personal routines that his wife and children necessarily establish during his absence. New found interests have been explored, and decisions have had to be made without the man of the house being around, and even well-intended interference is really not welcomed.

A diver working that routine needs more than a little Rest and Recuperation when he gets home. But it takes a thinking man to fully understand that in such case he is little more than a visitor, even if he *is* paying the bills, and so he wisely bites his tongue on many an occasion until he gets back to his own little isolated world where he may, perhaps, have a more legitimate say in what goes on around him.

Chapter Eight

A BIT OF THEORY

As the main subject of this book is divers, and not so much about diving, and the readers in the main will perhaps be those interested persons with little or no knowledge of the subject of diving (hence the attempt at simple though perhaps lengthy explanations) I think a basic description of the physical laws pertaining to diving and divers would not go amiss, along with a description of the various diving methods used. Hopefully this should give a useful background to those readers to enable them to more readily understand the diver's need for a thorough knowledge of his subject, and also of the kind of situations those divers later mentioned might have been involved in at any given time. Or, as later described, perhaps how it came about that they were exposed to certain fatally dangerous diving conditions and situations.

The English scientist Robert Boyle somewhere in his lifetime between 1627 and 1691, in research possibly related to diving, realised the importance of, and established the law which states that, the volume of a gas varies inversely with the pressure upon it if a constant temperature is maintained. (Boyle's Law). In other words, if our diver is breathing normal atmospheric air, as the pressure increases as he descends, the *volume* of the air he is breathing decreases proportionately, and though in our container, the diver, the *amount* of gas remains the same, as do the *percentages* of his breathing gas, in this case mainly oxygen and nitrogen, the partial pressures exerted by the gases in the mixture breathed will be increased as he continues his descent, as each gas, though mixed, retains its own individual presence, as shown in 'Dalton's Law'. This tells us that the total pressure within any mixture of gases is represented by the sum of the partial pressures of all gases within that mix. The effect of these two laws is assimilated right throughout the diver's body tissue, and the volume of his breathing media requirement therefore increases proportionately.

It follows that the air breathed by the diver will become denser, and it will readily be seen that the compression of individual elements of gases in the diver's body can, and do, give rise to increases in toxicity in various breathed gases, causing the likes of oxygen poisoning and nitrogen narcosis. It will become obvious also that the gas breathed will need to be given extended time to come out of his system, thus obviating the dangers of decompression sickness.

This all fits in very nicely with 'Henry's Law' which states that the amount of gas which dissolves in a liquid is proportional to the pressure of the gas exerted on the liquid, thus our diver, being mostly liquid, is subject to that law as we will later see.

Not all diving is done in deep water, but where it is the dive will call for some very specialised knowledge and attention to detail in planning, mostly on the part of the onsite diving supervisor, but also on the part of the diver too, though there are set routines which all of the diving team will be familiar with.

The diving contractor has supplied the men and equipment, and complied with all the diving and safety regulations pertaining thereto, as will have the installation manager. At the worksite the men have to put into practice what they have learned, both practically and in theory, and that can only be a combination of thorough training and practical experience, with more than a small sprinkling of lessons learned the hard way from mistakes made in the past. Like any job you might say, but with a difference here, as lives are at stake on a daily basis.

Using approximate measurements, on land at sea level where the atmospheric pressure is equivalent to about one kilogram per square centimetre, or one bar, (roughly fifteen pounds per square inch), for everyday purposes a person is said to be breathing a mixture of around twenty one percent oxygen and seventy nine percent nitrogen, but the nitrogen is nearer seventy eight percent, with traces of other insignificant gases making up the one percent of the total. We all know perfectly well that on planet earth, and for humans at various depths in waters within it, we need to breathe a correct mixture of gases, all containing at least some of the all important oxygen, to stay alive. This will be seen most clearly later in the book when two bell divers will be shown to have been supplied with neat, inert helium gas, and yet one's life was saved because he was able to pull off his mask and breathe air from the bell containing some oxygen, which saved his life.

Simplified, as we breathe in the air on dry land we take in the oxygen which, on reaching its destination - the blood capillaries of the lungs - takes part in an exchange of gases to displace carbon dioxide, a waste product of the blood which is passed back to the capillaries and thus out of the body as we exhale, when the capillaries once more take up the new oxygen supply as the process is repeated. The newly enriched blood is pumped around the whole body by the heart, and a continuous gas exchange takes place in all of the tissues of the body, as well as the lungs. The nitrogen, on land, being an inert gas, plays no part in this exchange, and is saturated in the body's tissues and blood. Around five percent of the oxygen is being absorbed and used in the body, and a slightly larger amount of carbon dioxide is breathed out. This is mostly taken up by plants in photosynthesis, one by-product of which is our user friendly oxygen. The remaining sixteen percent of the oxygen, along with the unwanted carbon dioxide, is also breathed out. The atmosphere around us remains basically unchanged however as the exhaled oxygen rejoins its mass, and the carbon dioxide diffuses to a miniscule atmospheric content of around 0.03 percent.

The body needs the oxygen to function normally, but in diving, both the oxygen and the nitrogen will become toxic under pressure, and the nitrogen can be replaced by other, non-toxic, inert gases. In the case of deep or sustained diving the inert gas used is helium, a gas second in lightness only to hydrogen that, for all practical purposes, is easier to breathe due to its lightness compared to other gases, and is neither toxic nor explosive. Helium is obtained from natural gas wells, and was first discovered in the sun's spectrum as long ago as the late 1860s, but was not found on earth until many years later.

The potential benefits of using mixed gas for deep diving rather than natural air were realised as long ago as the early 1920's when the United States Navy was experimenting with the use of mixtures of oxygen and helium, the latter being used in place of the nitrogen element in natural air. Not too long thereafter, in 1939, its use preserved the lives of many men during the first major operation of note using mixed gas when 33 men in the US Navy submarine Squalus, trapped on the seabed in 73 metres (240 feet) of water, were mercifully saved when a rescue bell - later known as the Squalus Bell (though properly known as the

McCann-Erickson Rescue Chamber) was positioned over and attached to the submarine and the men, survivors from the initial catastrophe, were able to transfer into it and were brought safely back to the surface. The gas was also instrumental in the diving that took place in the subsequent salvage of the same submarine, which was eventually put back into service.

I leave you to make up your own mind as to why, if the Squalus rescue could be accomplished in 1939, technology in the year 2000 could not have been mobilised in sufficient time to possibly save some lives in the Russian nuclear submarine disaster of August 12th when 118 men perished in the *Kursk* on the bed of the Barents Sea in a water depth by today's standards considered shallow for saturation divers at 100 metres. In fairness, however, in 75 submarine losses worldwide over the last one hundred years, the Squalus rescue was the only successful one of its kind, indeed in the whole of submarine history. Today, vast sums of money are being invested by Governments in developing high tech equipment for the very purpose of submarine rescue. Countries around the world such as the UK, USA, Germany, Norway, and Australia appear to have spared no expense on these very important developments, and are keeping pace with the ever greater depths to which the submarine may venture, even though, like any insurance policy, they hope never to have to use it.

In modern day recreational 'Technical Diving', various 'Nitrox' mixes are in use where additional oxygen is added to compressed air to increase the oxygen partial pressure of the mix, thus allowing divers to stay longer underwater with reduced decompression times, though sensibly it has been muted that the use of the standard diving air table to conduct decompression thereafter is the safer bet following such a dive. Some sport divers would probably consider this a waste of time, and defeating the object of the exercise, and I can see their point to a degree, but perhaps better to be safe than sorry. In the final analysis it's up to the individual, and proper training and sensible usage will win the day.

The British Royal Navy has been using various mixtures of nitrogen and oxygen in re-breather sets for many years, from as far back as the immediate post-war years of World War 2, but restricting their use to depths no greater than 55 metres. So, like the man said, there's nothing new under the sun.

In the past, various individuals experimented with potentially dangerous mixes of hydrogen and oxygen, which are explosive. It is well documented that a Swedish engineer, Arne Zetterstrom, was experimenting with such mixtures in the early 1940s.

Varying percentages of pure oxygen are added to helium depending on the depth the diver will be working at, and this mix will be monitored and modified depending on the circumstances dictated by the needs of the particular diving operation. In the early 1950s a depth of over 300 metres (1000 feet) was reached with a helium/oxygen mixture, though there is a significant difference between 'reaching' a depth and working comfortably and efficiently at it.

Helium is a rare and expensive gas, obtainable only in the United States and Russia, and has few drawbacks, but one of these is that breathing the gas distorts a diver's voice, though the reason for this is not properly understood, but can be overcome by the use of voice un-scramblers. The gas is also an extremely efficient conductor of heat, making thermal protection for the diver of greater importance than would otherwise be the case.

Pressure increases with water depth at a rate of approximately 0.22 kilograms per 30 centimetres (half a pound per foot), so that at 10 metres or 1 bar (one atmospheric pressure, equivalent to 33 feet of salt water) the approximate total, or *absolute* pressure, is double atmospheric pressure or 2 bar. It follows then that at 30 metres (100 feet) a diver is exposed to four times atmospheric pressure, at around 4.0 kilograms per square centimetre, 4 bar, (60 pounds per square inch), and so on down.

Serious problems can arise for a diver where air may become trapped in the body whilst he is surfacing under pressure. As the diver ascends, outside body pressure decreases allowing air in the body tissues and cavities to expand and sometimes become trapped causing tissue damage, often, but not always, causing great pain, and even paralysis or death if, for whatever reason, no decompression is carried out or is not exercised in a properly controlled manner. But even where it is, symptoms have been known to occur, even in the pub' after work, and need to be treated quickly.

This is decompression illness, or sickness, known colloquially as 'the bends', and can come from very painful joints such as the elbow or shoulder, or it can be very mild and known as 'niggles', and is not as unusual as one might think. This condition is classed as Type 1, which can also manifest itself as a skin rash with severe itching, but all of which can usually be easily cleared by a spell in a compression chamber breathing pure oxygen.

Type 2 symptoms are another story, and are exceedingly dangerous, though fortunately not so frequent as Type 1. These

Divers Compression Chamber

usually occur very quickly after surfacing at the dive site, and can manifest themselves as cerebral, causing possible stroke, or spinal causing paralysis, but without pain, and must be treated immediately if a chamber is available, which of course it must be in commercial operations. Otherwise for 'civilians' the Coastguard should be contacted right away to request immediate 'Medivac' to the nearest compression chamber as a matter of the greatest urgency.

It is not unknown for a diver to collapse on deck from paralysis of the lower body, or a blackout, or even to experience decompression sickness whilst still underwater, normally on a shallow decompression 'stop', and he can end up very dead or paralysed for life if the required treatment is unable to be administered in good time.

Unfortunately, not all diving operations are carried out under the strict rules of supervision of the commercial diving industry, or in compliance with the various Health and Safety at Work Acts, or Diving at Work Regulations, though even before they came into existence the first regulations relating to diving operations, The Diving Operations Special Regulations, 1960, revoked in 1981 (see 'Changes in Diving Regulations', page 184), laid down rules for the proper conduct of the land based 'working' divers' contractors. But, perhaps rather strangely, it is not in this type of operation where so many accidents or fatalities have occurred, even though there is more opportunity for 'acceptable risk' being taken in slightly *bending* (no pun intended) the rules.

Although this book is ultimately intended to show the diver fatalities that occurred at North European offshore sites in the latter thirty years of the twentieth century, and it is those kind of incidents that tend to attract most media attention, we should not lose sight of the fact that in addition to these, hundreds of lesser 'accidents' occur too, and many of these could have resulted in a fatality if it had not been for speed and skill on the part of those professionals involved - their own colleagues!

I am not in possession of accident statistics covering all of the years we are dealing with here in regard to diver fatalities, but in one ten year period, which I suppose we could call an average period offshore, from 1979 to 1989 in the UK Sector alone, though a regrettable but much improved 6 in number of divers died, in addition, 118 divers were involved in serious accidents where injuries were caused, including Type 2 decompression sickness, and 110 were involved in 'dangerous occurrences.'

It is an unfortunate truth that recreational divers have the world's worst record when it comes to such diving 'accidents', but these can almost always be easily traced back to the individual's lack of attention to detail or/and experience, rather than any lack of good club rules or maladministration; that is if the individuals actually ever belonged to a club.

The British Sub-Aqua Club and other suchlike associations have sound and professionally administered organisations, probably the best in the world given the comparatively tough diving conditions around our coasts, and it is a great pity that they are so often let down by the not so well-trained or well- equipped who sometimes make decisions when setting up a dive, or actually when diving, not at all in line with their own individual club policy or training methods. Although I realise that there are many more sport divers than there are professionals, one has only to browse the internet to see just how many amateurs literally get carried away by their summer madness, at much cost in time and effort to the emergency services, not to mention actual cost in monetary terms.

Diving From A Basket with Saturation Unit in the background

Chapter Nine

SOME TECHNICALITIES

The technicalities of diving have many facets, but can broadly be split into three different methods of approach for the ordinary, or perhaps not so ordinary, everyday working diver, if we ignore for the moment the wonderful innovations of one atmosphere suits, mini-submarines, and the like.

The generally utilised and approved commercial methods are; air diving, surface mixed gas diving, and saturation diving, all utilising surface supplied breathing media, depending on the type of diving undertaken, except where SCUBA is used in some adaptations utilising natural compressed air. However, because of its limitations, this latter equipment is now considered unsuitable for use in support of offshore oil and gas operations.

The choice of technique used for a particular dive or diving project requirement is determined by several factors. Mainly the water depth, as would be expected, followed by the amount of time required to be spent at that depth to accomplish any particular task or project, and the amount of decompression a diver would require on completion of each dive.

Natural air diving is the normal method used for water depths to around fifty metres (165 feet), and there are various kinds of launch and recovery systems for getting divers in and out of the water for all of the varying diving methods used.

For straight uncomplicated air diving the diver enters the water down a ladder, or by jumping in from a low platform or boat if he is familiar with the waters, or from a basket or skip suspended from a crane lowered to water level from high platforms, from where he descends to the required water depth to carry out his given task. Regulations ensure that the skip or basket and lifting appliance must be totally suitable for the job in hand, with room enough in the basket for two divers and their equipment; be secure against tipping or spinning, and be constructed in such a manner that its occupants are reasonably secure against falling out accidentally.

The diver is tended from the surface or basket by means of his lifeline or 'umbilical', the air supply hose and communications cable which can be made up in varying lengths, and even be of different colours for different divers if required, bundled together with a 12 millimetre (half inch) diameter nylon or polypropylene line for strength, and the diver's 'pneumo' hose, all taped together at about 60 centimetre (two feet) intervals to make a good, solid lifeline. Some diving companies make up their own umbilicals to their own requirements, but there are commercial companies who specialise in their manufacture for surface demand and bell diving applications, and others who specialise in their protection, with bend restrictors and flotation systems. When diving is taking place in deeper, therefore generally colder water, where hot water suits are worn, the hot water hose and other systems will also be enclosed within such a bundle, but these umbilicals are specially made for that particular adaptation.

The pneumo, or pneumofathometer, is simply a small hose of about 6 millimetres (one quarter inch) internal diameter, and open at its bottom end as it hangs from the umbilical at the diver's chest level, and at its inboard end is connected to a water depth gauge in the dive control station. At any time the diver is in the water, air can be blown down this hose by opening a valve on the depth gauge until the hose is empty of water, and when the valve is closed off the gauge indicates a back pressure equivalent to the diver's water depth.

On completion of his task, or when his recommended maximum 'bottom time' is up, (the time from leaving the surface to leaving the bottom), the diver is decompressed, if necessary, by surface control, either in the water only, direct to surface chamber, or a combination of both, (described as 'surface decompression') depending on the exposure to depth and the duration of the dive. This is accomplished by his doing some water decompression stops, if called for, usually at 3 metres (ten feet) intervals, leaving the water after his last stop, normally at 3 metres depth, and after removing his fins, if worn, at the bottom of the ladder, hurrying up the ladder onto the dive platform where he is assisted to quickly remove his helmet, weight belt and harness, and then, still in his wet suit and grabbing a towel, is hurriedly accompanied to the deck chamber and quickly recompressed by the use of air to the depth called for in the relevant dive table.

He will breathe pure oxygen supplied by mask, perhaps with the chamber O_2/CO_2 atmosphere being monitored, in a reasonably comfortable environment, for the time laid down in the particular dive table in use, and if the exhaled oxygen is not vented direct to atmosphere a system of venting and adding more air to the chamber simultaneously, thus flushing it through, is used by the operator to keep the chamber at the same pressure, which effectively keeps down an undesirable oxygen build-up in the chamber, and any increase of the inner temperature. This kind of use shows how essential it is that chamber operators should be fully trained and experienced.

If the decompression is to be prolonged his current novel, or cowboy book, will be waiting for him in the 'pot' (chamber), courtesy of the ever-attentive tender. Both heating or cooling can be applied, suitable lighting is mostly available and, safety being uppermost, on some chambers hyperbaric fire extinguishers are fitted, as it has been known in the past for older type chambers without external vents for exhaled oxygen within the chamber to ignite causing an internal conflagration within an oxygen atmosphere, perhaps from a spark from a defective light fitting. From there, after his decompression time is up, he will be brought slowly to the 'surface', or zero pressure, when he is free to take a shower, eat, and generally relax until his dive turn comes around again.

If the job has called for the use of 'tenders', the latter will assume responsibility for the diver's suit, his helmet if he has a personal one, and the remainder of the personal equipment used by the diver, and he will wash, clean, and dry these in readiness for that particular diver's next dive. Or if the tenders are general to the job they will jointly attend to all these matters in readiness for the next diver. If no tenders are on site then, of course, the diver will assume responsibility for his own equipment, and the ever-present need for tender activity is carried out by the other divers.

According to one particular Dive Table, so long as no dive was made in the previous twelve hours, an air diver can normally dive to 30 metres (100 feet) for one hour and need a total of 39 minutes decompression, whereas he can dive to 50 metres (165 feet) for five minutes and need no decompression at all, though a very steady rate of ascent is necessary of about 18 metres (60 feet) a minute.

It is exceedingly important, but very difficult, to judge an ascent speed from depth to the first decompression stop (if stops are called for) without any visible waymarks, but a tried and trusted method most easily accomplishes this by a reasonably slow and steady hand-over-hand one foot apart upward movement of about one second intervals. Surface control will be constantly monitoring the diver's depth by way of the pneumo gauge in any event, and will stop him at the required depths according to the stops indicated in the table used, or slow or stop him if the ascent is too fast.

Dive tables should never be memorised, so the bottom times given above are an illustrative example only, and in no way should be taken as gospel, but the example serves to show that the need for decompression is more dependent on the amount of *time* a diver is exposed to pressure as well as the depth of water.

In various countries throughout the world Mixed Gas diving directly from the surface, mostly by means of a diving bell, is utilised to depths of around 100 metres (330 feet), for projects of short duration where the diver will breathe a mixture of helium and oxygen, and decompression takes place in the water and in a surface compression chamber. This sort of diving utilises much the same kind of procedure as that later described for saturation diving, except that there is no habitat, i.e. the divers are not living in a chamber complex on the surface as later described, and the bell can either be closed or wet, when the diver can walk away after his decompression without having to be locked in a chamber complex for days or weeks on end as in saturation diving, as this 'bounce diving' system is normally used for short, but deep dives. However, in the UK a closed bell diving system should be used for all diving operations to water depths greater than 50 metres.

Fatalities have occurred in the past where the dive has been straight from the surface without a bell, whereas the presence of such a submersible chamber at the diver's working depth would have made all the difference, as it provides a bolt-hole for the diver if anything should go wrong, as later shown. The legal requirement for a submersible chamber (bell), to be on site, and utilised, has been brought into UK law by the very fact that divers' lives have been lost without one being available.

Diving bells have been around in some form or another for hundreds of years and were known in Greece in the 4th century BC, somehow resurfacing (if that is the correct word) in Europe in the 16th century, and were first recorded in England in 1620. But it wasn't until around 1928 when Sir Robert Davis came up with the Davis Submersible Decompression Chamber (SDC), with the ultimate intention in mind of eliminating the amount of time a diver has to spend underwater on decompression stops by transferring the diver from depth, whilst still under pressure, into a dry surface chamber. This of course would also leave the SDC free for continuation of diving operations.

This was the forerunner of Davis's Transfer Under Pressure (TUP) system which is basically the same system used today, except of course for more modernisation of transfer systems, instrumentation, and locking procedures. The distinct advantage of this system is obvious to all and, as with long exposures in air diving, the diver can ultimately breathe pure oxygen during decompression in the surface chamber to accelerate the subsequent overall decompression time which always, in any event, seems like an eternity.

Diving Support Vessel

Many rules and regulations apply to the use of submersible compression chambers, and all of the conditions therein must be fulfilled before their use is allowed. One of the most important being that the chamber must be used in association with stress tested lifting gear which enables the chamber to be lowered to the depth at which the diving operations are to be carried on, maintained in its position and raised, without excessive lateral, vertical or rotational movement taking place, and be provided with a means whereby, in the event of failure of the main lifting gear, the chamber can be returned to the surface. If those means involve the shedding of weights, they must be capable of being shed from the chamber by a person inside it, and a means must be incorporated to prevent their accidental shedding.

It will be seen here later the relevance of these regulations and how, once again, fatalities have forced their implementation following diver deaths.

As previously mentioned, for greater depths, or long-term exposure, a system called Saturation Diving is used, and it is worth, I believe, though at its most basic, explaining this method at some length. It is described as a procedure in accordance with which a diver is continuously subjected to an ambient pressure (the external pressure to which the diver's body is for the time being subjected) greater than atmospheric pressure, so that his body tissues become saturated with the inert element of the breathing mixture.

The deeper a diver goes on dives of long duration, the greater the necessity for prolonged decompression. It can therefore be clearly seen that on extended projects useful work time can be greatly reduced, and divers cannot remain in the water indefinitely, hence the need for a system such as saturation diving, again using mixtures of oxygen and helium supplied from the surface, where decompression can be delayed.

It has long been established that after having been subjected to increased pressure for between 12-24 hours, a diver's body becomes 'saturated' with the inert gas within the mixture he is breathing, so no matter how long he is kept at that pressure thereafter his decompression time will be the same. This very important fact is the crux of each and every planned saturation dive.

Expensive and technically complex diving systems known as Saturation Systems have been devised over the last forty years or more where a team of divers, monitored by a surface control team, can live under pressure inside a diving complex for long periods of time. These 'Sat' units, which might be up to 10 metres (30 feet) long, or even larger, consist of several chambers connected to each other by 'locks', or entry/exit doors, and must be large enough to allow a man to stand upright inside and live reasonably comfortably within it for many days or weeks at a time, with bunks, shower, washroom and lavatory, and changing facilities. They will be heated and well lit, and may even have piped music. They can be accommodated on the decks of offshore platforms, or

Divers leaving the bell at depth

derrick barges, or more usefully on a Diving Support Vessel (DSV), a vessel specially designed and fitted out for whatever diving project is anticipated, and can be utilised for both deep and shallow diving operations of long duration.

In this dry and stable atmosphere the divers, after each assuring their dive supervisor that they are well and fit to dive, are initially 'pressed down' in the saturation complex by the controlled ingress of various gas mixes of helium and oxygen to a mix which will ultimately be relevant to their 'storage depth', the approximate depth at which they will be working underwater. If the need arises, a final medical check can be carried out on the spot before the divers go into the complex.

The descent under pressure is carefully controlled by the topside crew to avoid the possibility of the divers suffering joint pains (Compression Arthralgia), which can occur if the descent is too rapid. On reaching the storage depth the whole complex is prepared and stabilised and, prior to the commencement of diving operations, a 'bell load-out' is carried out by the bellman by his entering the bell, which is at that time attached to the complex, and which will carry the divers down underwater to the worksite, when he will check out by communicating with the 'surface' crew that all the systems are functioning correctly.

On a two-man bell run, amongst other things, this will constitute two complete sets of diving equipment, the helmets and 'bail-out' systems, (the five or six minutes of emergency gas carried by the diver when he exits the bell). The umbilicals, which are coiled around hooks inside the bell, standard gas supplies, communications, demist system, hot water, various system gauges, and emergency gas supplies. It will be borne in mind that if any single one of these items fails to check out correctly the bell will not go.

As a simple generalisation the bell is a small, two or three man self-contained chamber clamped on top of, or at the side of, the main complex, depending on system design, and utilises a system for guiding it to the worksite or seabed by overhead gantry, with two guide wires attached to opposite sides of a five ton steel clump weight which is lowered to any required depth to keep the wires taut. When the bell (which has its own weight which can be released from inside the bell in an emergency) leaves the surface, it is suspended from a thick wire, the bell 'loadline', and the bell travels to the designated depth down the guide wires, just like a hotel lift, thus avoiding swinging about in aimless fashion, or rotating as it descends or ascends. In an emergency these wires can be utilised as a backup bell recovery system, but under normal operational conditions the clump and wires would be left in position until completion of all work, facilitating subsequent bell operations.

When all is ready, the first two divers will get suited up inside the chamber complex prior to entering the bell, where the diver intending to exit the bell will put on his harness, to which an umbilical will be attached containing all that is required to sustain him on his dive. His main gas system, communications, and hot water system is contained within the bell umbilical entering through a fitting on the bell from the outside, and this umbilical is controlled in and out from the surface on a winch drum. Weights are in the front of the harness, and the bail-out bottle, which is in a pouch in the harness on the diver's back, will be attached to his helmet by a thin hose.

When he is kitted up and ready to go, and the bell and accommodation hatches are all sealed, and all necessary checks have been made between the bellman and the topside controllers, the bell is detached from the main complex by the deck crew and, depending on layout of the spread, trolleyed over to the 'Moonpool', a hole in the centre of the deck of the diving platform, or over the side of the dive vessel, and put into the water and lowered to the working depth. On arrival at the designated depth, the inner and outer pressures will equalise and the bottom hatch will pop open. The bellman will then lift the hatch, fastening it back securely, and prepares his diver. If there is a little water in the bell it can be blown down by a slight increase of pressure within the bell once the diver has exited.

If not already done he will connect the diver's gas supply to the helmet, and then put the diver's helmet carefully on the diver's head. The bail-out bottle and hot water system will be connected, and the diver will get a rap on the top of his helmet or a thumbs-up in his window from the bellman to let him know that all is ready, and he can go. The diver will switch on the hot water to his suit, and then exit the bell, tended by the bellman, and go out to his worksite wearing boots or fins depending on the work involved, and the diver's discretion.

He is tended via his umbilical from the bell, and is in communication with the bellman and the surface, and the bellman, who will be dressed with only a need to put on his helmet in an emergency, will check his own separate gas supply to his own equipment which will remain in readiness should he be required to exit the bell at a moment's notice to go to the assistance of the first diver.

Emergency gas supply of the mix in use is readily available either from the surface or carried in tanks outside the bell, and can be piped through to the inside, and the diver will have with him his further limited supply of the same mix with which to bail out should his main gas supply be interrupted, or some other serious problem arise with the gas supply, to allow him sufficient time to reach the comparative safety of the bell.

However, it has occurred time and time again that, for quite inexplicable reasons, divers have failed to use this most essential piece of equipment to get themselves to safety and out of trouble. But then, at the penultimate moment of impending danger, who can say exactly what goes through any individual diver's mind, and who is to accurately analyse his last actions?

Besides voice communications, which are recorded, the surface Diving Control Room (DCR) can monitor the diver's movements and work progress if desired by video camera using a small Remotely Operated Vehicle which is put in the water by the surface team and sent down to the job, completely independently of the bell divers, and controlled by an operator in the DCR or separate nearby control room. The ROV provides additional bright light (the 'Snoopy' light) to that carried by the diver and can be made to follow the diver, allowing him to see well, and at the same time can send video pictures back to the DCR of the diver, or the job on which he is working, so that its progress can be monitored by any interested party such as a topside project engineer. The bellman can also be seen on a monitor in the DCR, so that nothing is left to chance, whilst he in turn is monitoring the various gauges within the bell

For the duration of the dive, a surface stand-by diver, depending on depth, (within the surface diving range), can be utilised to go to the assistance of one or both of the bell divers, and this diver is sometimes called for when the bellman is unable to cope with an emergency situation, perhaps with the man outside the bell as later mentioned in the death of a young American diver.

Some projects, in deep *or* shallow water, are run from a support vessel which is kept in position over the worksite by a Dynamic Positioning (DP) system (of which there are various kinds) whereby signals are received from seabed, satellite, or other types of surface fixed transponders by onboard computers. One type is known as a 'Taut Wire' system, where a wire with a heavy weight at its bottom is lowered over the side to the seabed. The surface unit contains the necessary instrumentation to detect changes in the angle of the wire and indicates to the computer the vessel's position, the computer making any necessary adjustments to this position.

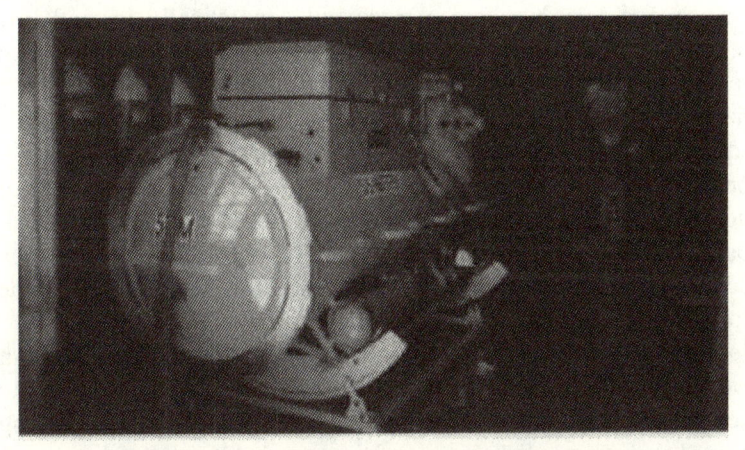

One-man Therapeutic Compression Chamber

The computers effectively control huge thrusters (variable pitch propellers) strategically positioned around and as an integral part of the vessel's hull, which cut in and out on computer command, pushing the vessel forwards, backwards, or from side to side to keep it in the exact required location. However, even though a back-up system is monitoring the 'online' system, occasionally things do go wrong, and any failure of the system can cause the vessel to 'run off' losing its position and, if divers are down, an exceedingly dangerous situation can be created whereby an abort procedure may need to be initiated. In the past, fatalities (as later mentioned) have occurred where a vessel has run off, but where, unfortunately, the abort procedure has failed them.

Meanwhile, inside the deck chamber, monitored by a qualified life-support technician, (saturation diving supervisors are qualified in life-support, but a separate person with this responsibility is desirable), the remainder of the diving team of men will live, breathe, eat, sleep (but obviously may not smoke) and attend to all their toiletries quite safely on the deck of the rig, barge, or other vessel, unless some unforeseen eventuality occurs.

An unforeseen occurrence took place with devastating results in the Norwegian Sector on the Byford Dolphin in 1983, in the north east Frigg Field, when the diving bell became detached from the complex whilst the system was pressurised to 92 metres (300 feet) with all the internal doors open. The four divers inside, two British and two Norwegian were killed practically instantly by 'explosive decompression.' It doesn't take much imagination to realise what a horrendous death this will have been, with gas at a pressure of 10 kilograms per square centimetre (150 pounds per square inch) deep within every tissue inside their bodies, suddenly being subjected to an outside body pressure reduction to that of normal atmospheric pressure of one bar, or 15 psi. This accident, once again, was instrumental in new regulations concerning certain refinements to bell attachment systems, and routines to be followed for the opening and closing of internal doors.

In any such event it is obvious that nothing can be done, but where possible disaster can be anticipated it would be essential to commence decompression procedures without delay, having regard to the extended amount of time needed to get the divers out. Sometimes though, even this is not successful, as happened in Singapore some years back when a typhoon blew up and the small barge on which the saturation unit was installed had to be abandoned, leaving the divers to their certain death when the barge turned over and sank. Their fate was either explosive decompression or drowning, but the former most certainly would have taken place as soon as gas connections were ripped from their positions. A similar situation occurred in the Gulf of Mexico with the loss of six divers, coincidentally, aboard the sister ship to the vessel used in the recovery of the gold bullion from HMS Edinburgh.

There are, in fact, survival systems whereby a chamber can be detached from its position on whatever deck platform it is occupying and launched over the side, complete with all that is necessary to ensure the divers are able to be brought safely to the surface, i.e. zero pressure, when recovered and re-established on a stable platform. There is also a one-man chamber which can be transported ashore by helicopter in dire emergencies, generally to the diver's own company complex where contingency plans will have been made for such an emergency. Unfortunately all installations and systems do not have this capability, though the divers will be quite well aware of that fact when entering the complex. Almost always decompression problems are resolved on site, but imagine the situation had divers been in deep saturation aboard the Piper Alpha platform!

Returning to our bell dive and the divers left in the chamber complex, as previously mentioned they can read, play cards, write mail or sleep, though on some kinds of dives, for specific purposes, a quiet period can be set aside for all divers to sleep rather than have a continuous work schedule.

Food, fresh clothes, books, mail, and even tools can be locked through to them by means of a small service lock on the side of the chamber. The breathing media in the chamber complex and bell, being a mixture of oxygen and helium, makes the divers' speech sound like Donald Duck and sometimes hard to understand, though modern helium speech unscramblers are a blessing.

The gas is carried aboard the diving platform, whatever that platform may be, in large colour-coded cylinder frames (quads) and the cylinders within are marked with the percentage mix, (or other gas) to avoid wrong identification. The gas is tested and delivered to the dive control system where it is set and monitored at a mix ratio pertinent to the depth at which the divers are working.

Gas pressure, percentage mix and purity, the chamber and bell temperatures and humidity, and the general health and well being of the divers are constantly monitored. Though the diver can be on an open circuit, that is, exhausting gas directly into the water, the expensive helium is normally returned topside from the diver by a vacuum system and 'scrubbed' of its carbon dioxide content through canisters able to absorb this unwanted waste gas, before being recycled back to the divers, thus saving on expense and the need to carry even greater quantities of helium. On a big job gas stored onboard can be millions of cubic feet. There are also carbon dioxide scrubbers in the bell and living quarters, and by this recovery process more than ninety percent helium reclaim can be achieved.

As breathing cold helium lowers body temperature quite drastically, and seawater temperatures can be very low, the hot water suits worn by the divers are essential and are normally worn over the top of thin rubber suits, the outer suit's hot water temperature being monitored at the surface at around fifty to sixty degrees centigrade, depending on outside water temperature, to give the diver a moderate temperature within his suit. The hot water passes through pipes between the layers of the diver's suit and is vented into the surrounding ocean at cuffs and ankles after doing its job of stabilising the diver in a comfortable condition. Heaters in the bell also function from this same system. Without this heat there is no way a diver or bellman could survive the cold at depth and, in the past, where systems have failed, diver fatalities through hypothermia have occurred. By the same token, hot water burns are not unknown, for instance on some systems, if the bellman turned his heat down, the temperature of water to the diver could increase.

When, in 1981, as previously mentioned, divers were working from the Dynamically Positioned recovery vessel *Stephaniturm* on the recovery of the £40 million of sunken Russian gold from the British Navy warship HMS Edinburgh, sunk in the Barents Sea above the Arctic Circle in 1942, 170 miles north of Murmansk in 245 metres (800 feet) of icy seawater, (2 degrees C.) the hot water for the divers' suits when leaving the surface was said to be almost at boiling point.

During his work when out of the bell a diver may 'excurt' up or down from the depth at which the bell is positioned, within certain limits. However, he may only move upwards from his storage depth, and then go down below it, but he cannot reverse that procedure, as he will then be subjected to unwanted decompression.

After a designated period of time the divers may exchange duties and, when any particular dive session is completed, the diver in the water will enter the bell from the worksite, and the then bellman, after assisting him in and taking off the diver's helmet, will close the hatch and slightly increase the pressure inside the bell, ensuring a good seal on the hatch before, once again, completing all necessary checks with surface control, when the bell will be drawn to the surface and locked back onto the main deck chamber complex.

The divers then lock through into the 'wet chamber' where they will strip off and wash their suits, and then shower and dress in clean clothes, probably thin cotton overalls, before entering the living quarters. Time to relax then, maybe eat a meal, catch up on the mail, or the newspapers if lucky, and almost certainly sleep after spending up to eight hours on the round trip. Divers change over, and the whole procedure starts again, 24 hours around the clock, subject to the conditions of the following.

The Health and Safety Executive Diving Information Sheet No7 dated 9/98 recommends however: " In order to ensure safe and efficient operations, it is important that diving personnel work with a time routine which allows them to develop a regular work and sleep pattern, and with a minimum rest period of 12 hours (i.e. not diving or carrying out pre- or post-dive checks).

Therefore, when bell diving operations are carried out around the clock, and on a continuous basis, they should be planned so that no diver takes part in a 6-hour lock-out operation, or an 8-hour bell run, more than once within a pre-planned 24-hour period."

In any case, because of high humidity, which is constantly monitored and automatically stabilised, and the relative high temperature, the chamber complexes are ideal breeding grounds for germs and fungi, so must be thoroughly cleaned by the divers inside at regular intervals using a special, non-toxic, anti-fungal preparation, and time must be taken to ensure that this is properly carried out. Divers will generally have eardrops with them to prevent an otitis type ear infection, which besides being extremely painful, can result in a diver having to be brought out of the complex altogether.

It may be imagined by the reader that the diver is working constantly on the seabed, and though this may be the case on some specialised units where pipeline maintenance or inspection is being carried out for example, in many cases it is not necessarily so, e.g. where divers are perhaps on board an installation almost purely for the maintenance of that structure and could therefore be working at any depth between surface and seabed.

All installations need to be inspected on a regular basis, and maintenance carried out thereto after intensive barnacle scraping, or water jetting, to enable the divers to inspect weld joints and various other connections and components such as Cathodic Protection anodes; sacrificial zinc blocks used to prevent corrosion. They may be working at a depth of say 60 metres with a water depth below them of 100 metres or more

It will be seen, therefore, that the whole unit is kept pressurised for the duration of the total task, which can take many days or weeks to complete. In the North Sea it is usually carried out on four week cycles when the crews change round and take their rest and recuperation.

Where continuous diving is required, dive complexes can have more than one set of work and living quarters so that diving can carry on without a break, but even without that, new divers can be locked through to replace, for example, a sick diver, or a diver having to come out for some other, perhaps personal or compassionate reason.

A doctor or medical attendant can also be locked through by way of an outer chamber within the complex to attend to any of the divers' various medical problems, if need be, or to take a look at a diver coming out with a medical problem. With the high humidity ear infections are not unusual, and some divers take in with them their own patent remedies. Decompression for those supernumerary entrants would then have to be commensurate with their exposure to time under pressure.

At the end of the current work phase, following a brief stabilisation period, decompression is commenced and, depending on the depth at which the divers have been pressurised, can take several days of mind numbing boredom, at what seems an interminable rate of ascent, before they are finally released from their virtual prison. Divers will tell you that this is the hardest, and seemingly longest part of the whole dive procedure, as the work is done and now there is nothing to do but wait, for days on end, until the moment of glorious release when pure, natural fresh air is breathed for the very first time since the day they were pressed down and, with a bit of luck, the North Sea summer sun will shine upon their pallid countenances, and some of those who swore they would 'stop smoking this time' light up their first cigarette for 28 days, as they head off home for a well earned break.

However, divers are normally required to stay within the near vicinity of a compression chamber for a specified time, normally twelve hours, in case the need arises for treatment for any subsequent arising decompression sickness; but after that they are free to go.

Normal UK practice dictates that if a diver has been in saturation for a continuous period of 28 days, the approved maximum time allowed, including decompression, it would be at least a further 28 days before he went back in again, so he has plenty of time to spend his well-earned money. A good gas diver who works regularly can therefore earn anything from £40,000 for six months work a year, and upwards of that depending on depth of water worked, so it's up to the individual to find the best employer with the best rates of pay. When you think about that seriously, one 28-day session in saturation will repay him an awful lot of money towards one gas diving course. Can't be bad!

Portable Gas Storage Tanks

Chapter Ten

THE FATALITIES

Although the seeds of oil and gas exploration activity were sown in the North Sea in the early 1960s, I have been unable to unearth any records of diver fatalities there prior to 1971. Those were very early days though, and having myself spent some years involved in oil and gas exploration in the USA, the Gulf of Suez, South America, and Australia, and being involved in several different methods of survey, and the utilisation of various kinds of survey equipment and accurate electronic navigation systems, I can well see that few fatalities were likely to have occurred in what I would call a fairly relaxed physical activity. However, that is my experience. What others have done, and what the extent of their physical participation was, I can only make an educated guess at.

Divers were only called on rarely if something went wrong with underwater snags or losses of equipment, and for most of my time, until something did go wrong, I was employed as a ship's navigator, utilising localised or worldwide navigation systems such as Decca or Omega.

Those early pioneers across the North Sea, the Dutch, first found gas in the now giant Groningen field in 1959, and it was all in their own territorial waters as the Continental medians had long been established, giving the British and Norwegians their own sides of the dividing line, too.

Although it's possible that accidents and even fatalities may have occurred in various sectors of the North Sea from 1959 until the start of the 1970s, it was in the Norwegian Sector that the first UK *recorded* fatality of a British diver came about.

This fatality occurred on the 1st February 1971, and I hope readers will not find the list of fatalities too repetitive, as, although the fatalities differ, and are interesting in themselves, lists are lists after all, though I have tried to intersperse items of interest.

Where 'installations' are mentioned in the text of fatalities this can mean a fixed platform, a drilling rig, a barge, dive support vessel, ship or boat, or any other vessel or platform capable of supporting a diving operation. Installations in brackets indicate a platform thought to have been used for a particular dive, but is not proved beyond doubt.

Michael LALLY

Although details in my possession of this fatal accident are scant indeed, on 1st February 1971, Michael (age not given) was a mixed gas diver who had been working in just over 60 metres (200 feet) of water, surface orientated (tended from the surface through his umbilical), from the semi-submersible drill rig 'Ocean Viking'. His cause of death was given as hypothermia and drowning, following a decompression problem, though how this actually came about does not appear in any records I can find. It *is* on record however that, "There was no diving bell" and " A bell would have been mandatory under UK current regulations." I have no idea when this report was first made out as those parts of the report I have in my possession are undated, but it was not until 1974 that any regulations, as shown below, applied to this kind of diving operational need for additional equipment to make such dives that much safer.

By today's standard 60 metres is not exactly classed as deep water, but this is most certainly one of the diver deaths which was instrumental in bringing about the beginnings of safe offshore diving practice regulations in as much as on 1st January 1975, the Offshore Installations (Diving Operations) Regulations 1974 came into being, wherein under the heading "Prohibited diving operations" paragraph 6(1) states, "It shall be the duty of the employers of divers and the diving supervisor each to secure that no diving operations are carried on, and the duty of a diver not to carry on any diving operation at depths greater than 50 metres (165 feet) unless, except in case of emergency, every descent to and ascent from the depth at which the diver is to work is made in a submersible compression chamber".

It is stated quite categorically by ex- Royal Navy Commander Jackie Warner, M.B.E; D.S.C, in his co-written book 'Requiem For a Diver', to whom I have spoken, and who was Chief Inspector of Diving under Tony Benn at the Department of Trade and Industry (later to become the Department of Energy) from 1974 to 1985, in reference to, though not naming, the above diver, and the next diver in this record: "I am convinced that, had a bell been mandatory at that time, neither diver would have died".

There are perhaps living today men who owe their very existence to Jackie Warner, who was instrumental in this over his years in office by successfully agitating for the introduction of many of the Safety Rules and Regulations now in place.

Tony Benn himself, who was Secretary of State for Energy as North Sea oil was being discovered, said in his complimentary foreword to Jackie's book, "... many lives have been saved as a result of his patient and persistent efforts to improve the conditions of divers as they follow their hazardous work, experiencing dangers on a grand scale."

Commander Warner was made an O.B.E in 1979 for his services to offshore diving, and retired from the Department of Energy in 1985.

Like all of the fatalities in this book, the actual physical causes of death of those who did die were known, but the *reason* for each death in many cases will always remain a mystery as the underwater life, and death, of a diver is a very lonely one, and who can say exactly what precipitated those last few moments of each terrible tragedy.

In the next diver fatality on *my* records, 'List of known Diving Fatalities...' etc, it shows that in the second recorded death of a diver in the North Sea, occurring on the same rig as Michael Lally, still in the Norwegian Sector but one month later, the diver was in fact in saturation and diving to the same depth, but using a bell. However, the full write up shows that he was not in saturation, or even a wet bell, so we can, I believe, safely assume that he was surface orientated, as was Lally.

There must have been much consternation aboard the semi-submersible drill rig 'Ocean Viking' on 1st March 1971 when this second British diver was killed just a few weeks later when returning from the same water depth as Michael Lally.

In 23 years connected with diving, in waters all over the world, although there were some near misses, I was never directly involved in a diver fatality. Those people aboard Ocean Viking must have been absolutely devastated to be involved in a second diver death so soon after the previous one, especially the diving crew, and most certainly the dive supervisor. Much more, of course, the deceased's family and friends who would have been doubly concerned for his safety, no doubt being fully aware of the previous fatality at his working location. This diver was Michael Brushneen.

Michael BRUSHNEEN

As stated, Michael, whose age is also not given, had also been working at a depth of 60 metres (200 feet) when he experienced a problem during decompression and was drowned having suffered a Pulmonary barotrauma resulting in Pneumothorax. Details, I am again sorry to say, are also very sketchy, except to repeat that he was also diving from the 'Ocean Viking' in the Norwegian Sector, presumably at the same worksite.

A bell would certainly have made for safer diving conditions, but as so often happens in the cases we will look at, although a cause of death can ultimately be established, the actual reason for all that took place with the diver on that day will forever remain a mystery.

Pulmonary barotrauma has been described for me by the Head of Diving and Hyperbaric Medicine at the Institute of Naval Medicine at Alverstoke in Hampshire as: " Barotrauma of the lungs. This usually results in rupture of the lung tissues with release of air from the lungs into the surrounding tissues. If the air is released into the potential space between the lungs and the inside of the chest a pneumothorax will be the result".

It can only be repeated that everything appeared to have been in order for this dive, but it would seem that any further attempt to solve the mystery of this fatality would only be conjecture.

Htun MINN (U HTUN MINN)

Htun Minn was British born on 21st July 1935, and was formerly a Lieutenant-Commander in the Burmese Navy, though having originally trained as an officer at the Royal Naval College, Greenwich, London. He later went to the USA where he trained as a Deep Sea Diver and decompression expert diving instructor with the US Navy at Norfolk, Virginia, having met his future wife Betty Nicholson in London, following which they were married in Rangoon, Burma. (Now Myanmar). They had two children, both born in Burma, Henry and Barbara. After leaving Burma he later obtained work with the Merchant Navy, but later again became Chief Diver for the world famous diving, and diving equipment manufacturer, Siebe Gorman, of Surbiton, Surrey. They lived in Lewisham, London.

On 1st November 1971, Htun, who was a fit and well thought of experienced diver, was working for Divcon aboard the drill-ship 'Glomar III' in the Central British Sector of the North Sea, 80 miles north-east of Aberdeen. He dived that day in 'Hard Hat' diving equipment, surface orientated and oxy/helium supplied, to a depth of 84 metres (275 feet). Having dived to the same depth on the previous day, within less than 24 hours he was back at work at the same site, apparently spending something more than forty minutes at the worksite securing lifting wire shackles to a damaged subsea wellhead which had to be recovered to the surface.

It would be the understatement of the last thirty-one years to say that the family does not agree with the conclusion of the official enquiry into the death of this diver on this day, especially in light of later discovered discrepancies in timing of events, and that the diving team appeared to have been a man short contrary to Section 7 (1) (a) of the then current Diving Operations Special Regulations, 1960, which stated quite clearly that "A sufficient number of suitable and competent persons shall be employed in attendance on him (any person employed under water as a diver) with a view to ensuring his safety." And especially as we are dealing here with a man of exceptional diving experience and ability in Hard Hat equipment. However, I can only state the official line known to me as to the events which *allegedly* followed.

It was reported that as Htun was ascending from the depth at which he was working his umbilical became tangled or caught up on some projection or other and he, quite naturally, proceeded to free himself. In the process of doing so, as far as is known, the fouled umbilical came free and an uncontrolled ascent was made to the surface where, according to the Aberdeen Coroner's report, he suffered an Air Embolism. He subsequently died in the deck compression chamber, though I gather that, under the circumstances, this recompression would, in any event, have had little or no therapeutic benefit because of the seriousness of the injury.

No bell was in use at that time as one was not required under the existing diving regulations. However, without a shadow of a doubt, even though no Diving Inspectorate existed at that time, the circumstances surrounding this fatality were significantly instrumental in recommendations being made towards the formulation and subsequent introduction of the aforementioned 1974 Offshore Diving Regulations which, as we have seen, made it illegal to carry out such an operation without a diver's bell.

Family dissatisfaction with the outcome of the Fatal Accident Enquiry held in the Aberdeen Sheriff Court by the Procurator Fiscal was never resolved, and it remains unresolved to this day why, amongst many other things, it is *alleged* that a very professional and well qualified diver experienced an uncontrolled ascent from depth sufficient to kill him. Not in the minds of the family however, as despite years of attempting to prove that gross negligence or acts or omissions were involved, I am told that none of their allegations were ever investigated. The family, and Mrs Minn's sister Jean Nicholson in particular, still vigorously continues with the sterling work jointly undertaken over the years in an attempt to prove a different case scenario.

On a personal note, Htun's son Henry "Chow" Minn who was born in 1956, and who has a daughter, Sorrel, also became a diver following entry into the Royal Navy in 1972, becoming a Petty Officer First Class Clearance Diver, as well as being the Light-Heavyweight Boxing Champion of the Navy at the age of 24 years. He was responsible for the recovery of many million dollars worth of drugs from beneath a vessel in Hong Kong in 1976, worked with the SBS, and was with N.A.T.O. During his Navy service he was also a member of the Scotland and Northern Ireland Bomb and Mine Disposal Team, (Later known as EOD,- Explosive Ordnance Disposal). Tragically, in 1986 he was discharged from the Navy as medically unfit following a devastating car accident when he skidded on black ice and went under a lorry, suffering a severe head injury resulting in Ataxia. He was in intensive care on life support, and is now disabled, and tells me he "lives in a wheelchair."

However, he can manage to get out of his wheelchair and into his motor scooter and get about with a reasonably good quality of life. He has also won Gold Medals for swimming at competitions for the physically disabled, but very much misses his former active life as a top class Navy Diver, as was his father.

I have no doubt that his father would have been as proud of him as he was, and is, of his father, and that though he was only 15 when his father died, Henry, at the very least, has the satisfaction of knowing that he did not die in vain.

Recognition of his mother's work is contained in a letter from The Department of Energy dated 23 July 1974, in which it is stated:

"However, it may give Mrs Minn some little comfort to know that the Government is in the process of introducing legislation on the safety, health and welfare of persons employed on drillships and other installations engaged in the search for offshore oil and gas. The legislation will, amongst other things, ensure that divers are given stringent periodical medical examinations, and that all possible steps are taken to ensure their safety at work."

Robert TAYLOR

On 1st May 1972, 25 year old Robert Taylor was employed by Strongwork Diving as a new British member of the diving team on the Drill Ship 'Britannia' located in Block 21 in the British southern sector gas fields of the North Sea.

Routine maintenance was being carried out in daylight conditions at a depth of 13.4 metres (44 feet) in reasonably clear water, with an underwater visibility in excess of 3 metres (10 feet), though again it is not stated if the work was on the seabed or at a mid-water point. Robert was initially acting as tender to the working diver, tending him from a cage which, as previously explained, would have been suspended from a crane to get the diver close to the surface of the water from a high platform.

The diver was underwater for 25 minutes, but did not complete the work on which he was engaged. As is usual, Robert, as tender, was the next diver, and dived using SCUBA, breathing natural air and free swimming, i.e. without a lifeline, to complete the job.

After 25 minutes he was given "visible and audible" instructions to return, (how, is not stated), but there was no response. The stand-by diver was immediately deployed but was unable to find any sign of the diver.

Robert's body was found some 11 hours later, tangled in a rope, and it was subsequently concluded that he had vomited and drowned, and the death was categorised as 'Medical', (Non pressure related). Again, what happened in those final moments no one really knows and, like many mysteries of the sea, no doubt this one will remain so also, though the report does mention the diver having had a large meal before diving, which surprises me, as it is a well known fact that divers are most careful to avoid that situation if there is the remotest chance they will be called on to make a dive.

However, it was also mentioned in the report that there was some doubt as to the diver's diving experience, upon which I cannot comment, but no doubt like all of us at times, he wanted to do a good job, and make a good impression.

Under Regulation 6. – (1)(b)(1) of the 1974 regulations which came into being two years later, in brief: " no supervisor shall allow and no diver will carry on any diving operation unless the diver at all times while he is under water is equipped with and securely connected to a lifeline or a breastrope which is connected to a person on the surface..."

A worthy hindsight of 20/20 vision which, when it was brought into law was, it is hoped, of some small consolation to Robert's relatives and friends as, once again, there is no doubt that this fatality was a prime mover in the instigation of the later legislation covering this type of diving operation.

Also, it is now recommended, as mentioned earlier, that SCUBA is no longer to be used in support of oil and gas operations.

P.J. (Paul) HAVLENA

This fatality occurred on 28 August 1973, aboard one of the then world's largest pipe laying and derrick barges - the 'L.B.Meaders', owned by the huge and many faceted American company Brown & Root, Inc, of New Orleans, Louisiana, which was working in Block 10 of the UK Central area of the North Sea.

Divers were in saturation, therefore on oxy/helium mix, and the depth of water they were working in was around 97 metres (320 feet). The dive on which Paul lost his life was a night dive, when two divers were engaged on "non-routine maintenance" work on a pipeline, both of whom were employed by the diving contractors Taylor Diving & Salvage Company Inc., of Belle Chase, Louisiana, USA.

Paul was a 29-year-old American and was the lead diver. His bellman, who was 28, and also American, was a diver called Helvey (first name not given in report).

As mentioned earlier, helium is a very expensive gas and, needless to say, diving companies are always looking for ways to save on the gas, hence the scrubbers and re-circulation systems utilised in saturation systems, diving bells, and divers breathing systems. On this dive, no doubt well known to the divers, a prototype reclamation system was in use.

Paul was working outside the bell, tended by diver Helvey, and was told to return to the bell as his working shift was completed. The diver, however, asked for permission to finish the job on which he was engaged, and was told that he could remain for another 15 minutes. However, one minute later, he said he was returning to the bell, but did not say why. He then asked for help from the bellman, who was immediately deployed, and who found the diver upside down beneath the bell anchor weight. The diver's air valve appeared to be shut, and it is reported that the bellman "thought he opened it." He could not get the diver back into the bell and a surface stand-by diver was deployed to assist, (remember this is 1973). The lead diver was got into the bell but was unconscious. Resuscitation techniques were carried out, but Paul died in the bell.

In his book 'Requiem for a Diver' Jackie Warner states:

"there is little doubt that the accident was caused by inadequate equipment design. This was a set-back to the helium reclamation goal, and only in more recent times has there been a general acceptance of the much more sophisticated helium reclamation systems."

The diagnosis as to the cause of death was established as Pulmonary Barotrauma resulting in a Pneumothorax.

Two things to look at here as perhaps being instrumental towards safe diving for successive divers in various operations of a similar kind - one is that diver's working times are now strictly controlled. The other is that the 1974 Regulations which came into force one year later made it compulsory that provision be made within submersible compression chambers for suitable lifting equipment capable of hoisting an unconscious or injured diver into the bell by a person within the bell. Note the word *compulsory,* as for some time previous to that date various companies had already been voluntarily and successfully operating with that very system. It may well have been the case in this fatality, but with the bellman being outside the bell it can be seen that he would have had great difficulty in getting a fully kitted diver up into it.

Once again the reason for what overcame the diver is not exactly known, but it would certainly appear to be something to do with his gas supply system, a fact which no doubt came out in the official enquiry, though I have not seen anything on this.

Timothy HOUSE.

Tim was a friend and colleague and, despite his age, was an experienced diver. We worked together, along with another diver whose name now escapes me, blasting a deep water harbour in Opporto in Portugal, in August and September of 1971, a couple of years before Tim's death. We worked for Strongwork Diving Company of Great Yarmouth, which I am told no longer exists. After the job was successfully completed, we went from Portugal back to the North Sea, and Tim was still there with Strongwork when he died on the 1st of December 1973. He was 24 years old.

I will not quickly forget that particular Portugal job as, apart from the enjoyable work and good companionship, I worked through the latter part of it feeling distinctly unwell, and was told by a doctor on our return that I had had a mild form of pneumonia. I was also told that my best girl friend had been sleeping with someone else during my absence. But, like I said, you have to be tough!

During our time there we worked through the nights, 7pm to 7am, as the locals used nearby beaches during the day and would not relish underwater explosions on their ears. The locals were also somewhat bemused to see us drinking brandy and beer at 7.30 most mornings, being our evenings of course, and some of them humorously called Tim, Timothy "Casa". We worked hard and had a lot of fun, and ate freshly barbecued sardines washed down with ice-cold beer in the bars on any evening we had downtime for bad weather.

We went our separate ways thereafter, and I was aghast when I heard that he was dead. I do not know, other than from hearsay, the intimate details of what happened, but frankly, knowing him as I did, have never believed that he cut his own umbilical, as reported. I have my own ideas of exactly what did happen on a rig moving up and down in a choppy sea with its anchor wires running through huge guide sheaves below the waterline but, even though it was a long time ago, perhaps it's better I keep those *exact* opinions to myself, though I can tell you what I heard at the time, and admit to being somewhat biased.

Tim was aboard the semi-submersible drill rig Blue Water III in Block 20 of the Central British Sector of the North Sea. The wind force was 6, about 24 knots (a strong breeze), so the water will have been choppy, especially as the water depth at which he was working was only between 4.5 to 6 metres (15 to 20 feet), though the water depth to the seabed was said to be around 150 metres (500 feet). This was a daylight dive using natural air, surface orientated, with communications, for the purpose of routine maintenance. No dive, to my mind, could have been more straightforward in concept, though dives in choppy shallow water are always uncomfortable for the diver's stability.

After about 15 minutes Tim was heard to be breathing heavily, when quite suddenly communications failed. The stand-by diver was immediately deployed, but found that the diver's umbilical was cut through, and there was no sign of the diver. The report said "It is *assumed* that the diver cut his umbilical, (an extraordinarily difficult thing to do under the best of conditions), in an effort to free himself having become tangled. Weights and wetsuit would then have dragged him down." His body was never found.

It is my opinion that no diving hose at that shallow depth with air going through it and no one on the end of it would stay underwater. In fact I heard that "it came fizzing to the surface." It was also later stated that because the water was a bit choppy, which meant the diver would have been tossed around a bit, he came up for another weight belt with which better to stabilise himself.

In addition, it was later stated by the diving inspector that, "his 'illogical action' was a direct result of Hypothermia. He had completed one dive that day and was shivering violently, (this may be when he came up for his second weight belt), but volunteered for a second dive to complete the task in hand." The inspector, very graciously, went on to say, "His actions reflect the professional pride of the offshore diver, who had to be rough and tough and wanted to see the job through."

Side door for locking on the Saturation Unit.
The Slip weights are in the bottom left of the diving bell

Per SKIPNESS

Robert John SMYTHE

At this time no full record can be found in the UK of this double fatal diving accident, though this is not uncommon because it came about in the Norwegian Sector of the North Sea, and as far as I can tell both divers were Norwegian, though I stand to be corrected on this.

Though I have received some helpful information from the 'Oljedirektorater' of the Norwegian Petroleum Directorate on several cases of diver fatality in the Norwegian sector, they have informed me that all the information concerning their diver fatalities I will mention here 'is part of a personal data register governed by the Personal Data Register Act' and that 'the information is subject to a duty of secrecy with reference to the Freedom Of Information Act, section 5, litra a, and the Public Administration Act, section 13, which refers to an individual's personal affairs', and they are unable therefore to give me all of the details which I requested on six different fatal accidents.

I understand and respect that to a degree, but not fully in view of the fact that in this country, the UK, such facts are public knowledge, and some of the accidents in Norwegian territory go back twenty to thirty years or more. It seems we must therefore go along with what information, and its presumed accuracy in translation, is available to me, having been grudgingly given, even though it has been pointed out that this is a tribute in an effort to establish a place in history for those who died, and not a macabre publicity seeking exercise.

Although I have fairly good records of most of the fatalities, it is sometimes necessary for me to delve into some of the cases already mentioned by Jackie Warner in his book, where he gives detail from the investigator's point of view, although in his day he himself was well known to the underwater world, both as a submariner of distinction, and as a diver of note.

The divers worked for the very respected diving company Ocean Systems and the client was Phillips Petroleum. The above fatalities occurred on 16th January 1974, in 76 metres (250 feet) of water during a bell dive from the rig Drill Master, when the bell suddenly surfaced with the bottom door open, resulting in the usual trauma to the bodies of divers in such incidents, causing both their deaths.

Mr Warner noted: " In the 1974 incident in Norwegian waters the ballast weights which keep the bell negatively buoyant were accidentally released, probably as a result of a breakdown in communications between the diving crew and the company's engineers in respect to modifications that had been made to the slipping device on the bell"

Since including Mr Warner's note, in my own later and more detailed enquiries I found more precise material confirming the above breakdown in communication by having a police report concerning the accident translated from Norwegian into English.

It would appear that the two men died simply because of a misunderstanding concerning an equalising valve inside the bell connected to the weight release mechanism, as to whether or not it should have been open or closed during the dive. The report is quite a technical and lengthy one following careful testing after the event and, in addition to it being hard for *me* to follow exactly, there is no real need to go into all of the finer detail here; sufficient to say that the instructions on board the Drill Master were not the correct ones for a system which had been modified since first installation. Because I have never seen such a system as was in use at the time of these fatalities, as far as I can reasonably gather in good faith from the report which I had translated into English - following the installation, a particular valve (Valve M) in question was documented to be closed in the instructions first given, but following the modification the valve was to be left open so that pressure on both sides of the bell weight release mechanism would, under normal circumstances, always remain equal; that is with the bell pressure on the spring keeping the mechanism locking rod in position, and the gas from a cylinder gauged and controlled by another valve from within the bell, equalizing the pressure from the other or outer side of the mechanism. Under the modified system, in the event of a leakage within the pipe from the bell side to the release mechanism the equalisation valve (M) inside the bell could be closed if required to maintain the bell's integrity. If the divers inside the bell *wanted* to release the bell weight, they could do so by increasing the pressure on the outer side of the mechanism by deliberately increasing the gas pressure by means of the relevant inner control, and closing the equalisation valve. There was, however, an unwanted leakage of gas into the outer side of the mechanism, and had the inner valve (M) been open, the pressure throughout the whole release mechanism would have remained equalised. However, the inner valve, as per the onboard instructions, was closed, and the gas built up within the outer side of the mechanism causing it to force the spring mechanism inwards, effectively withdrawing the locking rod, so releasing the bell weight.

It would appear from the report that Smythe had run a test on the system together with someone else and was told to ask Skipnes and another person about the use of the inner equalisation valve, but the other person mentioned stated that he was not asked and, of course, it will never be known if or when Smythe asked Skipnes about the valve.

From the same translated report, and here produced verbatim, we also have: 'But if one however just looks up in "Operating Procedures," it is not so simple to realise that the operating system for the locking rod is different. The instruction for dive on p.6 is clear: "Shut all valves." If therefore Per Skipnes had looked up in the available "Operating Procedures" and followed it, then all valves should have been closed, which they also were, which caused the accident. It is however unknown if Skipnes has looked up in "Operating Procedures" before the dive.'

Mr Warner commented that due to such unfortunate incidents as this becoming the subject of many of his submissions of diving memoranda, further such accidents were hopefully avoided.

This goes back to what I said in my preamble about many safety factors now in existence coming about purely because of such accidents. I made mention of the fact also that it is now incumbent upon all operators of diving equipment to ensure that, although a bell will have a system where the bell weight may be shed by divers from within the bell, the weight must be secured in such a fashion that its accidental release is not possible.

It is dreadful that men have to die before such safety factors are put into law, and I feel quite sure that, were it a son of mine who had died, I would want to know why these rules were not already in existence. However, this is the way of things, and has ever been thus, and we can only be grateful that others will not die because of those who perished before them.

My next review of a diver fatality is also to do with a diver's death in a diving bell, but horrific in the telling when one thinks of how simple misunderstanding between two divers of different nationalities can result in the unnecessary death of a competent and experienced man at the hands of an equally professional diver.

Mark BARTHELEMY

Mark Barthelemy was a 24-year-old Frenchman who died on the 11th April 1974. (A HSE Diving Inspectorate 'Diving Incident Report' in my hands also shows "Incident Date 01 March 1974?"). Mark was working for the French diving company Comex and was working out of a bell in just over 90 metres (300 feet) of water whilst saturation diving from the drill ship 'Havdrill' which was located and working in the British Sector of the South Irish Sea. His bellman, who was routinely tending him from the bell, was Scandinavian. The dive Supervisor was French, and the remainder of the support team were English, but all of whom spoke and were using English.

As I personally have scant detail of this "international incident", I will let the Diving Inspector at that time, Jackie Warner, again relate the story that came out following his investigation of the fatality:

" The diver lost his life as a result of a combination of errors, of that there is no doubt. The men were working at 300 feet, on the first operational dive, and there is little doubt they were out to prove themselves. The diver had left the bell and was at work, working very hard and observed by the diving supervisor on a television monitor in the dive control room topside.

His respiratory rate was high and the supervisor noted that he was working too hard. The diver was instructed to slow down his pace, but perhaps because of over enthusiasm, he ignored the request and worked to the point where he encountered respiratory fatigue.

He became unhappy and returned to the bell, the correct procedure in the event, but in his haste he failed to take the clear route back and passed on the wrong side of one of the bell weight guide wires.

The bellman, in his efforts to pull his colleague back to the interior of the bell, and safety, was in fact pulling the diver underwater, because the umbilical was wrapped around the bell weight wire.

Panic ensued, both diver and bellman reverted to their native tongues, and the squabble ended, unbelievably, with the bellman cutting the diver's umbilical, shutting the bottom door and telling the dive control to recover the bell to the surface.

When the bell was brought out of the water the body of the drowned diver was found draped over the bell weight.

The mental state of the bellman was such that any thought of instigating legal proceedings against him was ruled out as non-productive."

The name of the bellman is in my records, but its disclosure, as Mr Warner said, would be non-productive. Cause of death was given as above - drowning.

The Diving at Work Regulations 1997, Approved Code of Practice (ACOP) No: 60, now states that "The diving projects plan should state the language that is to be used during the diving project", although pointing out that in an emergency people do tend to revert to their native language.

A Pipe-Laying Barge

An offshore pipe-laying barge is not what the uninitiated might consider to be comparable to small long and narrow boats that run up and down canals. These flat-topped beasts are over a hundred metres long and more and are around thirty metres wide, sometimes bigger, and are worked virtually non-stop, 24 hours a day, seven days a week. Most are also construction barges with a huge crane at one end capable of lifting hundreds, some even thousands of tons, and one or two small deck cranes for lifting aboard pipe sections delivered to the lay-barge by smaller barges, and other small works.

In my day these barges were anchored with *eight* anchors to provide a stable platform for whatever operation was going on, either pipe-laying or construction work. The anchors were 'run' by the anchor handling boat, guided by the anchor foreman's radio directions, two to each of four corners, one each of which was positioned at right angles to the barge for lateral movement, and one each of which, for example, north west and north east at the front, as far out as the wire would reasonably reach with which to pull the barge forward, and south west and south east at the rear to be eased out as the barge moved forward.

All of this positioning took a considerable amount of time, and was never fast enough for the barge Captain, as his precious pipe was not being laid. But I remember one such Captain in Nigeria who gave me a few wicked games of chess in the interim, as we were obviously not diving at the time either.

These barges have danger around every corner, not just for the divers, but deck crew also. Pipe sections are lifted aboard, swung around on the crane, and stacked in a ready use rack at a convenient place on the lay-barge deck for later lifting to the 'line-up' station, the first position for each pipe section where, by the use of hydraulic rollers and other devices, it is lined up and touching the end of the previous pipe section.

The sections are about twelve metres (40 feet) long and wrapped in a special corrosion resistant coating such as coal tar enamel, and then a reinforced coating of about 10 centimetres of thick concrete (the 'weight coat'), and can be of various diameters depending on the job in hand. I have seen diameters of 142 centimetres (56 inches), though this was pulled off a beach, and that's pretty big! There is bare steel with bevelled edges at the ends of each section for welding operations that will join them together, known as 'field joints'.

As an example when laying pipe, in aerial view, the large crane might be to the rear, with the small crane and pipe sections at the front of the lay-barge. Running the length of the barge from front to rear at the right side will be a steel framework with rollers, along which are many 'stations' where various tasks are carried out. The small crane lifts a pipe section on to the first station and, when it is lined up as perfectly as can be, the line-up man strikes it with his hammer to let the root welders, top class men one on each side of the pipe section, know they can commence the first welding pass (the root) around the joint's complete circumference.

This operation is repeated, section after section over the course of a twelve hour shift, and as the barge pulls forward one pipe section length at a time, the pipe traverses backwards, stopping for each new pipe section to be lifted into place; at a guess about one every fifteen minutes.

It will be seen then that the root weld is now at the next station where the first 'filler' welders are located. They then put another weld run in on top of the root, the 'hot pass', whilst the next root is going in, and so on down the line. There are two or three filler stations depending on pipe diameter, and then a capping station, the final weld that will stand proud of the metal pipe before the next station, where it is x-rayed. Every single joint is almost instantaneously x-rayed and must pass muster. If it fails, the offending bad spot or spots are ground out, re-welded, and x-rayed again until all is well, the pipe moving on then to the next section, the 'dope and wrap' station, where the joint is wrapped in a flexible metal sheath and banded in position with a flapped hole in the top through which is poured boiling pitch. When filled, the hole flap is banded in position before the whole is ready to roll down the 'stinger' as previously described, and into the water. Surface inspectors check each wrapped joint for integrity.

If the inspector divers are smart they will get the dope and wrap crew to close and band each field joint flap in the same direction each time as an additional guide when carrying out underwater inspections on pipeline in conditions of poor visibility as, though field joints are normally numbered, being painted in large letters next to the joint, the numbers do get knocked about, and do wear off in time. If the diver can see or feel that the dope flap is closed, for example, from left to right facing the barge he will know which way he is moving as his inspection progresses.

As will be obvious, the forward movement of the barge is what makes the pipeline move backwards off the barge and down the stinger, and every pipeline move has to be co-ordinated. This is done with switches or push buttons on each work station so that the control man, he who co-ordinates the barge moves, will instigate the move once he gets a full set of green lights from all stations.

Nowadays there are bigger and better ways of doing all of this, with Dynamic Positioning and Satellite Navigation Systems instead of anchors and wires, but it will give the reader an idea of what takes place before the completed pipeline gets to lay on the seabed, hundreds of feet under the sea, and sometimes hundreds of miles long. Some barges are capable of laying many miles of continuous small bore pipe from a ready made-up spool, as well as utilising the conventional method.

It will be clearly seen that the pipe cannot just be left to hang over the stern of the barge, and this is where the stinger and our construction divers come on the scene. These are not the inspection divers, who work for the client and not the pipe lay company, and who inspect the line once it is on the seabed.

The stinger is two rows (imagine an upturned catamaran) of rigid or articulated pontoons with rollers in the middle and at the sides down which the pipe will run. The profile of the stinger, sometimes hundreds of feet long, must be maintained by a combination of automatic control and diver intervention, in a soft contour down to close to the seabed, its end six to ten metres or so above the seabed, whilst the pipe is eased out down the stinger, held back with tensioning shoes at the stern of the barge, as the barge moves forward.

Much simplified, the pontoons have air pipes connected to them, and vent valves on top, and it is necessary for the diver to move up and down the stinger for inspection or correction of the profile, by letting air into the pontoon tanks or venting off where need be to maintain that profile. At the far end of the stinger there is a pneumo hose with which to monitor its depth from onboard the barge.

The ideal diving equipment for this job would be SCUBA when the diver could zip up and down at will, though this would be possible only in fairly shallow water, but today, of course, SCUBA is not recommended for use in our offshore industry, for very good reasons, and there is deep and dark water to consider, and much danger.

Divers are surface orientated, and herein lays great danger of fingers, arms and legs, or umbilical, being caught up or crushed by moving rollers or pipeline, as well as the danger from suction on opened valves. A lot of the stinger profiling is done automatically and is overseen by topside engineers, but divers do need to go along its length, and probably more than on most jobs need to be extremely vigilant as the job, especially if done in the dark, or in murky water, is one of the most dangerous underwater inspections a diver can undertake.

The underwater pipeline inspectors, the client's divers, confine their activities to inspecting and reporting on the condition of the line on the seabed, mainly to check that it is lying properly, that there is no broken weight coat, and that there are no unsupported spans, which must be sorted later by the construction divers by packing the unsupported sections with sandbags of grout. Field joints, as stated, are normally numbered so that everyone knows exactly what location is being talked about should any later remedial work need to be carried out. One not insignificant danger when swimming a line is to be suddenly smacked in the face by a piece of broken, (when the pipe is rolling down the stinger), unseen stainless steel field joint banding sticking vertically upwards.

Laying pipe can be very interesting or boring work depending on how you are made, but I always liked it and found it interesting and, just to stay amused, when not diving, used to go around the various work stations in an effort to help out, fetch tea for chess playing welder mates, or try to learn something about the other people's work.

William NORRIS

Bill Norris, whom I knew, worked on such a pipe-laying barge, although it was not directly responsible for his death, as it most certainly has been for many other divers in various parts of the world.

Bill was a 40 year old British diver working in the British Sector of the North Sea when, on 30th March 1974, he surfaced after being taken ill at 200 feet and complained of feeling unwell when he came up. He died whilst being treated in the deck chamber on the lay-barge and, although I want this book to be of good memories of divers who died, I have to be brutally honest here and say that Bill was actually assessed after the occurrence as being unfit through health to be diving anywhere, and had he been examined by an approved doctor under the later introduced UK offshore medical guidelines laid down in regulations he would not have been passed as fit to dive.

A post mortem observed by a Dr Calder of Royal Marsden Hospital, London revealed that he was medically unfit to dive and as a result suffered a form of decompression sickness, though the type is not specified in reports that are currently available.

A saving grace of the apparent cause of this fatality, of course, is that it no doubt contributed to the stringent rules laid down that very year in regard to the requirement for Certificates of Medical Fitness under the 1974 Diving Regulations. This states that no diver will be employed to dive unless he is in possession of a valid medical certificate, that is less than twelve months old, from an *approved* doctor, issued after examination, and stating that that person is fit to dive and that the certificate is valid for the diving operations in question. In addition, the Regulations state that if a diver is unable to work underwater through accident or illness for a period of more than seven days, his certificate will no longer be valid until he has seen an approved doctor once again and been certified to resume his underwater duties. It's a fact that there is light at the end of every tunnel, and in his own way Bill did his bit towards safer diving for all those coming along behind.

John DIMMER

John Dimmer was a 27 year old British diver employed by the Diving Company K.D.Marine aboard the permanent platform Sedco 135F located in the British Sector of the North Sea, and on 5th July 1974, was in saturation with other divers at a depth of 150 metres (492 feet). The report does not specify on what type of underwater bell work the divers had been engaged, but during decompression John suffered a pneumothorax, which is when the breathing media leaks through from a lung into the chest cavity. It is not known why this sometimes occurs in a perfectly healthy man but, on decompression, when pressure is decreasing, gas trapped can suddenly burst through the lung, collapsing it.

Pneumothorax is a serious condition but, uncomplicated, need not result in death if properly treated. It requires the cavity to be vented and for an equal pressure inside and outside the affected lung to be maintained until the decompression is complete and the diver is at the surface.

It should have seen the preservation of John's life when the Diving Supervisor immediately recognised his symptoms, but unfortunately for him the doctor with whom the platform made onshore communication, and who was apparently untrained in diving medicine, despite having the condition described to him by the experienced supervisor, "failed to recognise the symptoms of a classic case of pneumothorax in a known pressure environment", and gave his own wrong diagnosis as pneumonia, giving instructions to the supervisor to proceed to treat the diver as such.

The supervisor was obliged to take the doctor's instructions and continue decompressing the diver…who subsequently died.

This was a diving fatality that could have been so easily avoided and, after a post-mortem carried out in Aberdeen by a Dr Hendrey, strong 20/20 hindsight vision was invoked in recommendations being made for the need for specialised medical advisors in this field.

So once again we come to the situation where someone's death was necessary before the door was closed so to speak, the horse having bolted, and like the UK divers in the early days of North Sea oil who had to feel their way, so too did the administration, right up to government level, before they got it right.

Not long after that we got the *approved* latter-day doctors who are specialists in, or at least familiar enough with, diving medicine, even though there existed a British Royal Navy Physical Laboratories for diving medicine a million years before North Sea oil was ever dreamed of. Deep water diving had been going on in Government controlled oil and gas territory for years before the introduction of suitable regulation, and it was not until the first, and later Chief Inspector of diving, Jackie Warner, came along to plug all the gaps that something was done about it and, in his own words, " From the early 1970s we did build up a dossier of information from fatal accidents, and we moved towards drafting regulations which did, in the end, help cut the death toll significantly."

Gas storage tanks

P. KELLY

I am sorry to say that I do not have the first name of this British diver who died on 27th August 1974, the result of a most unusual and rare unprofessional occurrence whilst working on an installation in the Norwegian Sector of the North Sea. Fatalities or accidents in that sector were not within the jurisdiction of the UK Diving Inspectorate and are not therefore recorded fully within the realms of that organisation, at that time the Department of Energy. Mr Kelly was in the process of bell diving to around 92 metres (300 feet) of water when pure helium was fed to the two divers in the bell as it descended.

As described in previous pages you will realise that helium is an inert gas, as is the nitrogen in our atmosphere, and without a certain percentage of oxygen mixed with either of those gases when being breathed we would very quickly lose consciousness and eventually die.

Both divers were wearing breathing masks, as the bell atmosphere was air, which would normally have been dangerous to breathe at working depth but, however, saved the life of one of the divers because it contained a small percentage of oxygen.

Both divers passed out quickly on a pure helium supply through their masks, but one pulled off his mask before becoming unconscious. He collapsed, but he was breathing air from the bell's atmosphere, part oxygen, which saved his life. Diver Kelly died from anoxia (no oxygen) due to inhaling pure helium.

It was reported that there had been a failure in communications when ordering the gas, and that the Diving Supervisor did not test the gas before use, though how either failure could have come about is absolutely beyond the comprehension of anyone to whom I have spoken about the matter. The Approved Code of Practice is now that pure helium should not be used in diving operations except as a calibration gas or for a specific operational requirement, and that a small percentage of oxygen, normally 2%, should always be present in helium.

Referring back to some Technical Matters you will recall that all gas quads and the gas cylinders within them are, quite logically and sensibly, marked with their contents and percentage mixes by the gas supply company, but this particular fatality proves that they don't always get it right, so in future supervisors must always check those contents and mixes to make sure they are absolutely correct. For many years the various gases in bottles have had distinguishing markings or colour codings, so what went wrong on this particular occasion is another of those enduring mysteries. It is now the responsibility of diving contractors to ensure that all gas storage units comply with international, European, or national standards of colour coding of gas storage cylinders, and the contents must be checked on receipt and also immediately prior to use.

It can clearly be seen emerging now what I said in earlier pages that most preventions to accidents that are now in place are the result of accidents and fatalities that have happened in the past, though unfortunately costing divers their lives on the way.

I must stress once again though that all the connected industries throughout the UK, whether on or offshore, are ever alert in matters of safety and safety training, and the encouragement of safe practise is second to none throughout the world.

J. K. J. CLARK

Again I am sorry to say that I have only this diver's initial and family name on my record, and this is the fatality that I mentioned earlier when indicating how quickly and easily a diver could lose his life, often in what might appear to be the least likely of circumstances.

This British diver was 31 years of age, and worked for the well-known and respected French diving company Comex. When he lost his life on 14th October 1974, he was working in Block 24 of the Central British Sector of the North Sea from the semi-submersible drill-rig 'Waage One'. No water depth is given in this report as the accident leading to his death occurred on the surface of the water.

This was a night dive, and two divers were in the water apparently employed on 'non-routine maintenance', attempting to attach a marker buoy to an anchor. They were both wearing SCUBA and breathing normal air, and were not attached to each other.

The water was choppy and, as I have said previously, some surface jobs in these conditions, besides being tiring, can be very dangerous for a diver when getting thrown backwards and forwards by the waves and washed into the structure or metal projections.

This particular diver was actually monitoring and acting as stand-by from the surface for the underwater diver and was washed into a surface obstruction, and it was later assumed that it was at that stage, or a combination of that and the recovery stage, that he suffered broken ribs. The second diver came to his assistance, and he was towed back to the diving basket, quite a distance of around 20 metres (65 feet), but his mask had come off and he drowned. Apparently he had also vomited, and though resuscitation was commenced it was to no avail.

It is a sad fact of life that this diver would have benefited from the regulations that came into operation the following January, just over two months later, that no diver will enter the water unless being securely attached to a lifeline and has a means of communication with the surface or another diver. And though it may have been academic on this occasion, those same regulations made it compulsory that a diver's light must be carried in such circumstances, and the surrounding area must be brightly illuminated.

Not personally being very tolerant of apparent repetition in written works I would be the very first person to admit that lists are sometimes mind numbingly boring unless a person has a really deep interest in the subject to hand. Fortunately for me in this particular case I do, and I sincerely hope that this will be the case with the reader, as there really is no other way to tabulate a list of 58 diver fatalities and the circumstances surrounding their deaths in as much detail as one can muster, especially as we are talking here of a special historical tribute to these men.

As has been repeated so often, without divers the oil and gas revolution that most of us experienced during the last thirty years or so of the 20th Century could never have taken place. You may equally well say that about the drillers, the geologists, and the engineers, and a myriad of others also, whether losing their lives or not; hopefully not, and it is my sincere hope that perhaps one day someone better informed will write up a definitive history of the whole of those years covering all aspects of the professions involved and the contributions they made. Those years were historically important years and are deserving of a very special place in the history of the development of our oil and gas industries and the consequent redevelopment of our nation.

When one looks at the overall situation it is almost beyond belief that not for hundreds, or even thousands, but for millions of years, oil and gas bubbled beneath the surface of our own backyard. It wasn't suddenly ready to use like the kettle with the hot water for your cup of tea, it was ready for exploitation thousands, maybe even millions of years ago, but it took until our very own lifetimes to find, and to develop the technology to exploit, what had been lying there all that time. So too the moon, and getting to it and back again, and other wonders of our technological age, and we have been so very fortunate to have lived in this most productive of times and been able to be a part of it all.

No doubt in fifty, or even perhaps a hundred years hence when (I am convinced that with ever improving technology our oil will still be with us) divers could be routinely working thousands of feet beneath the sea, perhaps in dry one atmosphere titanium habitats, and they will wonder how we did what we did with the, by then, Stoneage equipment that we had!

Alternatively, though, a recent report tells of a huge discovery of oil in the Caspian Sea off Khazakhstan with an oil-bearing structure 120 kilometres (46 miles) long, in a water depth of *3 metres* (10 feet). No! That is not a misprint. Not much depth pay on that job! Though with winter temperatures at minus 40 degrees Celsius, I wouldn't think there would be too many applicants.

At the opposite end of the scale, installations already exist in deep water where the hand of a deep-sea diver has never set lead boot or fin, nor is there any need for him to do so. The BP operated Foinaven, Schiehallion/ Loyal fields west of Shetland lie in water depths of between 400 to 600 metres (approx 1300 to 2000 feet) and 350 to 450 metres (approx 1150 to 1500 feet) respectively, and all are heavily reliant on unmanned intervention where, due to the great water depths, completions are sub-sea, and oil is produced through rigid flowlines and then brought to the surface by means of flotation supported flexible risers into floating production, storage, and offloading systems, which are utilised rather than fixed platforms. The oil is then exported to terminals in Orkney and Shetland by tanker shuttle.

Gaining that kind of accomplishment in such an environment took over twenty years of hard work and perseverance from 1972 to 1992 before the first commercially viable discovery, Foinaven, was made, and the field began production in 1997, followed by Schiehallion in 1998. It is already anticipated that BP will be investing a lot more in this area, especially in the Clare and Magnus fields.

It has been reported that worldwide expenditure is set to double within the next five years in waters exceeding 300 metres (1000 feet), especially around South America and West Africa, so there is every chance that improving technology will expand the UK's horizons ever north and westwards, and it is forecast that investment in the North Sea in 2001 could be as much as £4 billion.

BP, the world's second largest oil company, is currently looking to increase its annual investment to £9 billion worldwide in places such as Iran, China, Angola, Trinidad and the Gulf of

Mexico, and Chief Executive Sir John Browne has already said in relation to the North Sea, "Investment will rise significantly next year."

All in all, whatever the outcome, surely nothing like this can happen again to have the same monumentally seismic impact on all our lives and the country's economy as a whole that this glorious black gold has done. Black North Sea gold, or "Texas Tea," as it's known down south. But then again, who knows?

The very day following the death of British diver J.Clark in the British Sector of the North Sea another fatality occurred, but this time in the North Sea's Norwegian Sector. It was on the 15th October 1974, and by the most awful coincidence for the diving company involved, as this British diver also worked for the same French diving company, Comex. He was:

Gary SHIELDS

Gary was but a boy, but doing a real man's job at the tender age of 21 years. He was not the youngest diver to lose his life over the years in the North Sea, but pretty close to it, and it was whilst working as a bell diver, a top qualified man, on the Ekofisk Pipeline from a Diving Support Vessel (Oregis).

What an absolutely thrilling and interesting life he must have had at such a young age. How his contemporaries must have envied him his lifestyle, and what a future he had ahead of him; but it was not to be.

Gary was working on an unspecified task from saturation on an oxy/helium gas mix in a little more than 73 metres (240 feet) of water, and had been doing so for around two hours, but then returned to the bell to ask for another 'strop'. (A continuous loop of wire used to place around an object, generally for lifting purposes).

At that time surface support decided to change his gas supply to a new bank, and as the diver returned to his worksite he found that he could not breathe, suffering a loss of main gas supply, and began a return journey to the bell. Unfortunately, perhaps because he was in a desperate hurry, despite having with him an emergency supply of his breathing gas, his umbilical became fouled and he could not reach the safety of the bell.

Nothing is mentioned about his bellman, the stand-by diver, only that there was a 'suspected communications failure.' The report does not say with whom - surface to diver, surface to bell, or bell to diver or vice versa, but in any event Gary died right there of asphyxia. For some inexplicable reason he did not use his emergency supply of gas, as has happened in many other cases, and none of us know why except to say that when one breathes out quite normally and breathes in again but nothing is there, just what is the next move? Logically, being well trained you go straight to your emergency supply as you move swiftly back to the bell, but then other circumstances can come into play and who knows what goes through the diver's mind from that moment on?

Nothing is mentioned either of any repercussions as a result of this fatality, in my opinion a totally unnecessary death, though as I said earlier, I am not in possession of all the facts on all of the cases. As I write, this death was 27 years ago and I repeat that modern day databases were non-existent. As I write also, Gary would have been a mere 48 years old, perhaps with a wife and grown up children, and no doubt retired to sunny Spain!

To reprise, we are still in 1974, the very worst of years for diver deaths in the North European sphere of oil and gas operations, when ten divers lost their lives. Seven of them were British, two Norwegian, and one French, though two of the British were in Norwegian waters, and the one Frenchman was in the British Sector. This was the year of the first big Regulation for divers and diving operations generally, but the next two years were to be little better on accidents when a total of eight divers lost their lives in 1975, six of them in the British Sector, and in 1976 a total of nine more diver fatalities occurred, all in British Territorial Waters.

David KEANE

British diver David Keane was one of the odd ones out, losing his life on an installation in the Irish Sector of the Celtic Sea, on 2nd December 1974. Once again I do not have the diver's age, nor the depth of water in which he was working, but as he was working from a bell we may consider that his depth was substantial, though it was not stated if the bell was wet or closed.

What is known is that the weather was bad, and the diver's umbilical was cut through, and it is thought that an up and down movement of the bell had caused it. However, there were apparently no previous complaints from the diver or the bellman concerning the bell movement until the latter suddenly realised that the diver's umbilical had been severed, "probably by the movement of the bell against some underwater obstruction." The foregoing is a supposition, and I feel therefore that I might be allowed an opinion. I personally find it very hard to believe, as it would have taken little or no effort on the part of the topside crew for the bell to have been re-positioned, unless for some obscure reason the bell just had to be where it was which, to my mind, would have caused all kinds of unwarranted damage to the outside of the bell and its ancillary equipment such as emergency gas supply tanks, and would have been totally unacceptable.

Again, and quite incredibly, the diver did not use his emergency supply of mixed gas, and was reported to have lost his life to asphyxia through drowning.

J. PHILLIPS

Unbelievably, our next diver also worked for Comex, who by this time must have been getting distinctly edgy about their divers who were employed on various North Sea oil and gas diving operations, although this is a worldwide and vastly experienced professional diving company.

I personally have worked on contract to Comex in the past and know them to be a good and reliable company, but things were certainly not going well for them towards the end of 1974. The diver on this particular project was the above-mentioned J.Phillips, (no first name given again), who was British and 30 years old.

This particular fatality occurred on the 17th December whilst the diver was working from a jet barge at Scapa Flow in British Territorial Waters, classed as in the Northern Sector of the North Sea, in just over 30 metres (100 feet) of water. The work involved was again classed as "routine maintenance" and was categorised as a "Structural Failure" but in the same report, was detailed under another heading of "Accidental Fitting Disconnection". Yet in what little text there is available a further statement reads that the fatality came about as a result of a valve being knocked off a pipe by a jet sledge. Remember, the diver was working from just such a vessel. Jackie Warner, the Chief Diving Inspector at the time states that "sometime previously, a valve on the line had been damaged" and then surmises "possibly by a vessel's anchor cable or by a fishing boat's trawl doors."

So, where are we? This is the HSE's Incident Report resume from the official report made at the time:

"The diver was working from a jet barge on a pipeline on the seabed at Scapa Flow. A valve was knocked off the pipe by the jet sledge. The resulting suction, atmosphere to 100 feet of seawater, sucked the diver into the 20 centimetre (8-inch) valve opening, killing him instantly. The stand-by diver was deployed but could not recover the body immediately."

No diving equipment is mentioned, either for the diver or his stand-by, but obviously the surface knew there was a problem when it mobilised the stand-by diver, so it can be assumed, as many things are around these fatalities, that there was some kind of communication, which failed, thus alerting the topside crew.

No mention has been made as to whether or not this jet barge was working burying pipe, its primary purpose in life. At the time of the above fatality, but perhaps improved today, pipelines could be buried comfortably in water up to around 60 metres for the purposes of protecting them from the likes of anchors or fishing trawls. At the best of times, working from these jet barges is exceedingly hazardous. The jetting nozzles used can put out pressures of up to 1000 psi, and the suction hoses used to pick up and throw out the spoil can be around 30 centimetres (12 inches) in diameter or larger, and are not to be approached, whilst visibility is often nil.

Very simply, the sledge is like a big heavy saddle often weighing more than one hundred tonnes, with rubber rollers around its perimeter so that it may sit down over the pipeline, suspended by wire rope from the barge, without actually damaging the pipe. Attached to the sledge and pointed towards the seabed beneath the pipeline are the powerful jet nozzles which blast down into the seabed to the required depth, whilst the sledge suction hoses pick up the spoil and throw it to the sides; or it may be recovered to the surface for disposal. The sledge is dragged along the pipeline at a speed depending on several things, mainly the depth required to bury the pipe, the makeup of the seabed material, and the power of the machinery itself.

I imagine that the valve mentioned above was an existing pipeline valve previously installed for a tie-in to another line at some future date, and these normally have to be protected by some kind of guard. It was perhaps this guard that was being removed by the diver when the valve broke away, and yet the HSE report says that the sledge knocked the valve off. I can't imagine for the life of me what the diver would have been doing in front of the sledge, so close that he was sucked into the valve when the sledge hit it? The position of these pipeline valves are known, and the jet barge is normally stopped before it gets anywhere near the valve prior to necessary preparations being made to jet through it.

The mystery that we have here seems to have been made by confusion of record keeping once again rather than one known only to the diver!

I can only complete this by saying that the following year Regulations were made under the Petroleum and Submarine Pipelines Act 1975 on a number of subjects concerning the health, welfare and safety of pipeline workers, including diving operations and inspectors.

Need I say again that perhaps once more we have *some* good coming out of a fatality, though again of little consolation to the next of kin of this diver.

John MARTIN

This was a case of another lost diver, but also emanates from a very poor partial report in my possession, so I will do my best to make some sense out of it.

The fatality occurred on 6 February 1975, in the Stavanger Fjord, Norway, when 30 year old British diver John Martin, who was working for the well-known diving company Ocean Systems, from an unnamed Diving Support Vessel (Condeep), at around 43 metres (140 feet), and in clear water, with a seawater temperature of less than 5 degrees C. The seabed depth at that point was 244 metres (800 feet).

The diver was surface orientated and breathing compressed natural air, though no equipment is described. He was working on a 'construction project' when he asked for his slack umbilical to be taken up. On a normal diving operation this could mean that the diver's tender had let out too much and the slack was pulling on the diver in a tide or current movement. On the other hand it could mean that the diver was about to leave the worksite to start an ascent, though this would normally be preceded by some kind of verbal communication or statement to that effect.

Some kind of communication was made, but whatever it consisted of was soon lost and the tender began to pull up on the diver's umbilical. It is reported that at about 22 metres (70 feet) the umbilical went slack and was pulled up with no diver at its end. It was 'assumed' that the diver had detached his safety clip by mistake; presumably the one that attaches his umbilical to his harness or belt, and this would put a direct pull onto the diver's mask or helmet.

More assumption comes into play here when the report continues that the diver's mask was dislodged, but he held on to it whilst being pulled up, but his airline fitting became detached as the diver reached almost surface level, ("1 foot") and the diver's body sank to the seabed.

A surface stand-by diver was deployed but no sign of the diver was seen, and his body was never recovered. Death was recorded as drowning, but the reason given was 'slipped helmet...some evidence of Nitrogen Narcosis'.

The accident was categorised as 'Personal equipment failure/problem' and the incident characteristics were given as 'Lost diver-parting of umbilical-accidental fitting dis-connection'.

The one final thing that was said in this report under comments was 'Suspected lack of training', but quite where that came into the equation is not explained.

Kevin WILSON

Kevin Wilson was one of the youngest divers ever to die whilst working in the North Sea, at the tender age of 20 years. I say die rather than lose his life as he did not lose that short life to diving as such, but to natural causes. In other words medical rather that pressure related, though no doubt exacerbated by the effort expended on the work on which he was engaged, although this was classed as inspection work which is not normally very physically demanding.

It came about on 1st March 1975, when a team of divers were working for Cue Diving Ltd aboard the permanent platform 4927B Leman. That is Quadrant 049 in Block 27 of the UK Southern Sector of the North Sea.

Kevin, who was British, was at a depth of around 43 metres (140 feet) in SCUBA with a 'buddy' diver and they were working around the legs of the platform measuring for *scour,* the amount of seabed washed away from around each leg leaving the leg standing in what looks like a deep circular bowl. After a short time on the bottom, Kevin started to swim upwards towards the surface, and no doubt being surprised at this, his buddy started to follow him, as it would be normal to let the other diver know if you intended to do something unusual.

Within a very short time however the buddy diver noticed that something was wrong with the first diver and went to his assistance. He aided the diver to the surface and called out for help, but the diver was apparently too heavy for him to support and they both started to sink The buddy therefore "ditched Wilson's breathing apparatus." Help arrived and the troubled diver was recovered to the platform, but all attempts to revive or resuscitate him failed.

The cause of death was given as Pulmonary Oedema caused by Cardiomyopathy. The former means excess fluid within the lungs that reduces the ability for them to function. The diver would feel short of breath and perhaps start to cough, and this no doubt was the reason that Kevin headed off so quickly towards the surface. Cardiomyopathy is a disease of the heart muscle that results in the heart being unable to function efficiently. It would appear that the diver had an inherent heart disease that had not been detected in any medical examination he had had prior to going out to the worksite.

One wonders if SCUBA had not been in use on this particular dive, as of the previously mentioned recommendations of the HSE, if the end result would have been any different? But I personally think that in the final analysis it would have made no difference.

The inevitable final word was that the diver had died from natural causes.

A. L. ALVESTAD

This diver was Norwegian and 30 years old, and was employed by a Norwegian company called 'Three X' on the 'Borgny' Dolphin in Block 21 in the UK Central Sector of the North Sea. This was a drillship which was positioned in 140 metres (460 feet) of water.

A team of divers were in saturation on 22 March 1975, and outside the accommodation the wind was Force 4 giving a kindly moderate breeze of around 14 knots, but with a cold sea temperature of about 5 degrees Celsius.

The bell was down and the work on which the diver was engaged was again classed as routine maintenance, yet it was known that he had deliberately made himself heavy with extra weight to enable him to carry out the hard work the task evidently required. He had been working out of the bell for approximately 20 minutes when both voice and lifeline communications ceased. The bellman acting swiftly went out of the bell and recovered the first diver back into it. The bell was then brought to the surface by the normal method and locked on to the saturation complex when diver Alvestad was got into the chamber complex interior where mouth-to-mouth resuscitation and heart massage were carried out, but to no avail. The diver was pronounced dead, presumably unofficially by the divers inside.

Apparently the diver's heating system had failed and he was breathing an oxy / helium gas mixture without any external or respiratory gas heating, which obviously meant that he would have been very cold. Factors expressed in this fatality stated that the diver had died of a non-pressure related medical condition by a combination of hypothermia and hypoxia through overwork, though it was known that the oxygen content of his gas was correct for the mix in use.

Of academic interest, I have two reports from the same source, one of which says that the diver was 30, and the other that he was 31. More to the point, one report gave a contributory cause of death as Anoxia, and the other as Anoxia/Hypoxia. Anoxia is a complete lack of oxygen, like diver Kelly, above, who was fed pure helium, whereas Hypoxia is a *reduction* in oxygen supply to tissue or the whole body, so one might say that both reports are correct in as much as the Hypoxia no doubt led on to the Anoxia.

Dr Hendry of Aberdeen (whom I believe carried out the post-mortem) commented that by his overwork the diver probably beat his own ability to take up oxygen, which in some mild form or other I think most divers have experienced at one time or another. The extreme cold that the diver experienced through heating failure, and breathing helium in cold-water conditions, was without doubt the reason for the sudden onset of unconsciousness, deepening to death.

George TURNER

The loss of this British diver was another mystery of the sea which will forever remain thus, and yet again this was a diver with the French diving company Comex. It is also a catalogue of mixed diving equipment, mixed gases, and mixed emotions when *three* stand-by divers, one buddy and two others, were taken ill in some form or another, and one diver died. An event which must surely only take place once every hundred years, and especially as the next reported diver fatalities in July of the same year, both working together on the same job, were also in the hundred year cycle.

To set the scene, this was a daylight dive that took place on 14th June 1975, from the Construction/Pipe Laying Barge 'Choctaw 1', located in the Norwegian Sector of the North Sea. Two divers were to dive together, stated to be surface orientated, and who "chose" to dive in SCUBA.

(A line of text in one report, from an official source, said the dive was using a mixture of helium and oxygen, though the facts later in the report seem to refute this).

Diver Turner, (no age given), was to dive to 50 metres (165 feet) along with his buddy, (although it would appear they were both attached to the surface by lifelines), to carry out a survey of the seabed, which was at 69 metres (226 feet), apparently to locate dropped items.

A pipelay/derrick barge does not have legs down which the divers may traverse, and no mention is made of a downline, or shotrope, so quite how a 'survey' leaving 19 metres (over 62 feet) of empty water between the intended maximum depth and the seabed, using two divers, was to be carried out can only be a matter for conjecture. I know that underwater visibility in the North Sea can sometimes be quite brilliant, but I never imagined it could ever be that good!

The dive commenced and at 50 metres, the maximum intended depth, the buddy diver felt ill and returned to the surface. Not long thereafter diver Turner's lifeline went slack, and his tender thought that he was surfacing also, but on picking up on the diver's lifeline he found that there was no diver at the end of it.

A stand-by diver was immediately deployed (type of equipment or breathing media is not given) and he too became ill.

A fourth diver, using surface supplied 'air', was quickly deployed and he found and recovered the first diver's body, though he suffered Nitrogen Narcosis at some stage during the recovery.

All attempts at resuscitation of the first diver failed, and it was subsequently reported that he had drowned. It was also subsequently reported that the diver had died as a result of his own actions under the influence of Nitrogen Narcosis, and had slipped his lifeline. But once again that is supposition as no-one knows the real truth, and never will, though giving credit to the diving inspector in the depths that we are talking about, and the divers' using natural air, as was obviously the real breathing media, there would appear to be no other decision that could safely be reached.

Nitrogen Narcosis, known in the old days as 'Raptures of the Deep', can occur at any depth after the doubling of atmospheric pressure, but usually kicks in at around 25 to 30 metres if it is going to do it early, and there is nothing very rapturous about it at all.

It is not understood exactly how it is caused, but it is obviously related to the increase in the partial pressure of the nitrogen exerted as the diver descends. The feeling is a mixture of emotions depending on the individual concerned, and never particularly manifests itself in the same way twice, or to different people. It can be a feeling of dizziness, or drunken euphoria, of fear and disorientation, or of reckless bravado, and must be recognised for what it is immediately. The normal way of dealing with it is to stop descending and come back up a little until it clears, which it invariably will. Going back down then will almost always show it to have cleared sufficiently, or perhaps completely, and if an effort is then made to think clearly as work is progressed the dive can be perfectly successful. I often found that a month's leave could make me quite water unfit as far as clearing ears and a bit of narcosis is concerned, but you are soon back in the swing, and in discussions on the subject I have found that the same kind of reaction to a lay-off period in other divers is not at all unusual.

Unfortunately, though the onset of the narcosis can sometimes be quite sudden at deeper depths, and this is when it will hit the hardest, it is sometimes impossible to control before it takes over the mind completely, sometimes with fatal result.

Previous to the above fatality, on 6th February 1975, an unknown Dutch diver was said to be about to commence a welding job in 14 metres (45 feet) of water somewhere in the Dutch Sector of the North Sea, when he just disappeared, and subsequently no body, even in that shallow depth, was ever recovered.

This incident is on record with the UK's HSE, but the Staatstoezicht op de Mijnen (Dutch State Supervision of Mines) who have answered all my queries on lost Dutch divers, has no knowledge of any such diver.

Peter WALSH

Peter CARSON

In this double diver tragedy one can only feel horror at the death of these two men who, in the penultimate moments of their lives were in possession of full certain knowledge that they were going to die, and could do nothing about it. But mercifully, a third diver in the identical situation was spared the loss of his life, and for that, being one of our own, we must all be eternally grateful, as no doubt he will be until the end of his days.

These fatalities occurred in British Territorial Waters in Scapa Flow on 6 July 1975, when the two above mentioned British divers, the latter being 20 years of age, were working on a pipeline, in good visibility, in around 37 metres (120 feet) of water. Classed as an inshore location, they were working for a company called Underwater Security Ltd from an 'installation', probably a vessel, the 'Celtic Surveyor'.

The pipeline on which the first diver, Walsh, was working was of very large diameter, and no indication is given as to what type of diving equipment was in use, but I imagine in those early days and in the depth given it would have been SCUBA. Apparently the operation was to 'pig' the line, and the pig was being pushed along the line by air pressure.

It somehow came about that through "a lack of appreciation (or knowledge ?) of the differential pressures" inside and outside of the pipeline, when the valve was opened, the diver was sucked into the pipe. The first stand-by diver, Carson, was got swiftly into the water, and he too was also sucked into the pipeline.

The hardest part of this story to believe is that one would have thought that by now someone would have noticed that there was something dreadfully wrong, and that someone in the topside crew would have been alert to what was happening, yet a third diver was sent down to assist and he too was sucked into the pipeline.

The merciful side to this whole sad episode is that, by now, the pressures inside and outside of the pipeline were equalising and the third diver, with great presence of mind, and one might say also of a commendable wish for self preservation, was able to get out by removing his breathing gear (but still using it to breathe), turn around and swim out from the pipeline.

As with diver Phillips, mentioned earlier, no doubt these deaths had a huge impact on the industry as a whole, either precipitating or demanding amendment to the 1975 Pipelines Act in which divers and pipelines were together considered.

Roger BALDWIN

Peter HOLMES

This double fatality was unusual in that it was not on an actual dive that the two divers met their deaths, but in what should have been the relevant comfort of a safe, warm and reasonably comfortable chamber complex following a perfectly successful bell dive from saturation, breathing oxy/helium.

The divers were working for Oceaneering, probably one of the most famous and well established diving companies in the world, and especially offshore, and the project installation was the Waage II, a semi-submersible drill rig located in the northern British Sector of the North Sea.

The date was the 9th September 1975, and the water depth in which the two British divers had been working was about 120 metres (390 feet). Roger Baldwin, a 24 year old ex-Royal Navy diver, who I understand had purchased his release from the Navy especially to go into oilfield diving, and Peter Holmes, who was 29 years old. The dive was apparently for the purposes of inspection, but of what is not stated. It *is* indicated however that Baldwin was the lead diver, with Holmes as his bellman, though on this particular occasion those facts were of academic interest as the two men died together following an accumulation of errors and wrong interpretation of information.

A pressure leak appeared to have been observed by the supervisor on the complex during decompression, and helium was added to compensate for the loss, when the internal temperature increased. The divers began showing signs of extreme distress, as the chambers are always kept at high temperature anyway to welcome invariably cold divers back from the depths. For some reason the Control Room Supervisor was unable to relieve their condition, even though the divers themselves would normally have been able to pass back through into the cool of the wet chamber that they both first entered from the bell. Both divers collapsed onto the floor of the chamber and another diver was locked through into the complex to assess the condition of the divers, but found them both to be dead.

It would appear that the whole ongoing saga was down to human error on the part of the supervisor who, for some unknown reason, which no doubt came out at the ensuing enquiry, had been monitoring the bell pressure and not that of the chamber complex master gauge.

The post mortem found signs consistent with heat stroke, in fact the opposite of hypothermia that our modern day society now talks so much about, sometimes found in sick elderly people. Hyperthemia, too much heat, had made the divers collapse and die, and the deaths were recorded as such.

Apparently this was the first recorded case of such a cause of death, although it served, once again, to underline the importance of keeping divers in an oxy/helium atmosphere in safe thermal balance.

John HOWELL

'Scouse' Howell, as he was known to his friends, was also an ex- Royal Navy diver, a 'Clearance' diver or 'Corkhead' as they were humorously known to us 'Steamers', the hard-hat, big boots brigade of the Navy diving teams. Highly trained over long periods of time, and in murky, cold and dark conditions, these divers were, and still are, trained in the Navy specifically for the work of what is now known as 'Explosive Ordinance Disposal' (EOD), which was at one time known as 'Bomb and Mine Disposal.' Training also includes underwater engineering, saturation diving, and salvage, so diver Howell was no slouch when it came to experience and an ability to put out a good job of work.

My own brother 'Blondie' was one such, a Chief Petty Officer Diver, and later Warrant Officer, who was instrumental in the training of many Navy divers, and was himself a prime mover in the subsequent recovery of sensitive Government documents and instrumentation from the wreck of HMS Coventry after it was sunk during the Falklands war in 1982, for which he was awarded the British Empire Medal, having personally led a team of divers into this dangerous wreck in 98 metres (320 feet) of water.

This was accomplished using a similar system of saturation diving technique herein used by Scouse, who had made the transition to civilian saturation diving, and I am grateful to my brother for his input to this book in explaining salient points of this system to me.

Scouse was 25 years old, or should we say *young* about these divers, who never really got off the ground, so to speak? He was working for Sub Sea International Offshore aboard the 'Western Pacesetter', yet another semi-submersible drill rig, and this one was positioned in Block 10 of the UK Sector of the Northern North Sea.

It was a cold and miserable night dive on January 12th 1976, and this was accomplished using a bell to dive to 146 metres (460 feet) in icy water, breathing a relevant oxy/helium mix, to re-establish guide wires to a wellhead.

It would appear that the diver partially passed out soon after leaving the bell, and it was later assumed that he had knocked off his own breathing supply of gas just before leaving, though I have seen no actual documentation as proof that this was ever definitely established. Again this assumption is contagious, but as has been said all along, when the divers are there and we are here, who really knows what went on once all the panic dies down, equipment has been handled and moved around, and memories are somewhat dimmed?

In any event, a small recovery must have been made, as the diver then struggled to get back to the bell and was pulled up by the bellman, but was again unconscious after a huge effort was made to get him back inside. No attempt was made, once again, on the part of the diver to use his own emergency gas supply, and subsequent resuscitation did not succeed.

The final Diving Inspector's report was that in attempting to breathe he *might* have broken the seal on his helmet and inhaled water.

The incident duration took place over a two hour period before final recovery to the surface was made, and the final categorisation of the diving fatality was that the diver had succumbed through 'personal equipment failure/problem causing shortage of gas, resulting in loss of consciousness leading to death by drowning'.

It is now recommended by the HSE that the gas supply in a diving bell should be designed in such a way that, if the main surface to bell umbilical pressure is lost, the bell onboard emergency gas is brought on-line to the diver or divers.

Clay ELLIS

This American diver was another 20 year old who never got to live long enough to enjoy any of the rewards of his chosen profession, losing his life in what could well have been another tragic double fatality, through no fault of either diver, though we have here too, a second diver being very seriously injured indeed. These kinds of accidents should never be able to happen, but again we are talking of 25 years ago when bell systems and their operative mechanisms were not up to today's high standard.

The incident date was just five days after diver Howell died, the 17th January 1976, when two divers were to make a 'bounce dive' (more or less straight down and back up again) from the supply boat 'Smit Lloyd 112', which was stationed in quadrant 030, in Block 24, in the UK Sector of the Central North Sea. The diving company was again Comex.

The dive was to be from saturation to 77 metres (253 feet) for the purposes of non-routine maintenance, and it is not stated how long the divers had been in saturation, nor how many divers were in the complex. The bellman was a 29-year-old British diver, D.A.Bannister, and the system in use was a buoyant bell where the bell is actually floating at depth whilst the bell weight sits on the seabed some little way beneath it. This system can be used to effect where there is a sea swell, and when properly monitored the up and down movement of the bell is effectively curtailed, or at the very least, minimised.

Apparently the bell had to be moved, and it is assumed that drag on the bell weight across the seabed, or suction from the seabed, was too much for the bell guide wires and attachments and there was a serious equipment failure. The bell weight tray was ripped off causing the bell to immediately surface in the space of one minute, completely uncontrolled, and with the bottom door open.

Clay Ellis, although subsequently recompressed, died, whilst diver Bannister surfaced with serious injuries. He was transferred to hospital after therapeutic decompression, where his condition was said to have improved, though later Jackie Warner in his previously mentioned book said that the man was left almost completely paralysed.

It would appear that the loss of the bell weight was caused by the fracture of the eccentric pin on the starboard side of the bell, and the mechanism on the port side was badly bent allowing the weight tray to become detached from the buoyant bell.

The pathologist in the case of Ellis was Dr Hendry of Aberdeen, and both men, not unnaturally, had suffered massive lung Barotrauma, with embolism and resultant Pneumothorax. One lived and one died. Who can account for it?

Anthony (Tony) DOBSON

Anthony, or 'Tony' Dobson was a British diver who worked for me as his supervisor on Kharg Island in Iran when we were both employed in the Middle East in the 1970's. We worked on the installation of the then world's largest oil pipeline riser, and I knew Tony to be a good and reliable diver. If I remember right, he had made the transition from being a hotel chef, and was more than well pleased to have qualified as a professional diver.

He was 30 years of age, and was killed on 3rd May 1976, which would not be long after he left the Middle East, and I was astounded and much saddened to hear of his death.

He was working from the construction and pipelaying barge 'Orca', in quadrant 47 of Block 8 in the Southern UK Sector of the North Sea, the 'Rough Field', and was yet another diver employed by the French company Comex. He was surface orientated on a night dive, on air through an umbilical, and the maximum water depth was 36 metres (120 feet).

Working from a pipe lay-barge is dangerous work at the best of times, and hideously so at night when one is totally unaware of the exact position of a trailing umbilical, valves, pipe brackets and other projections running the full length of the stinger, and especially if the barge is progressing; which it could be, though as this dive was from a basket, and inspection work was to be carried out, it would not logically have been on the move.

It is always a good idea to try to get a look at a stinger before it is submerged, in an effort to familiarise oneself with the layout of this monster, which can sometimes be hundreds of feet long, depending on water depth. But this is often not possible if joining a barge during an ongoing project, and then again things take on different shapes and sizes at night, and it would not be beyond the best of divers to become disorientated and get fouled up on such a beast.

It is not stated exactly what the inspection and non-routine maintenance work that the diver was working on was, but my guess is that he was carrying out a stinger profile check, and perhaps adjusting buoyancy here and there, as on a lay-barge that is mostly what one is there for, as well as monitoring the pipe down onto the seabed.

On this particular night the work was well out along the trailing stinger, so much so that the dive subsequently required decompression, and of course the diver had to swim out and down a long way to get out to the site to perform his task.

On being recalled to the cage he had trouble with his umbilical, which was hung up somewhere. By now the tide was picking up, but the diver reached the cage safely and was raised up slightly, only to find that his umbilical had fouled again and he was obliged to return to sort out the problem as he obviously could not be raised any further with things as they were. He was then brought up to 12 metres for his first decompression stop of 15 minutes, following which he was raised to 9 metres for a 20-minute stop. By the worst of bad fortune his umbilical had fouled again, but he stated that he thought he had enough slack to reach the surface. The basket was raised to the surface but the diver was pulled out of the basket by the still fouled umbilical, and swept away.

The stand-by diver was immediately, dangerously, deployed in the fast running water, but was unable to recover the diver back to safety; the total duration of the dive and attempted rescue taking well over two hours.

It was apparently impossible to attempt any further rescue bid thereafter until the tide had eased, at which time Tony's body was found with his mask off.

The pathologist, Dr A.Harrison of Great Yarmouth, later confirmed that death was due to drowning.

N. HUBERT

No first name is given for this diver, nor any subsequent one until the penultimate death in 1996, and the last diver to die in the British Sector of the North Sea in the 20th Century. For some reason the use of first names was discontinued in subsequent HSE Dive Incident Reports.

One week after Tony Dobson died, another British diver, N.Hubert, who was 24 years old, lost his life diving in Loch Fyne in Scotland, which is not North Sea territory but on the Scottish west side above the Isle of Arran on the Argyll and Bute coast. This is an arm of the Firth of Clyde, originally famous for its shipbuilding, but now equally as famous for the construction of offshore oil platforms.

This, of course, is classed as inshore UK, and the installation was 'PT One Elfa Norge', another construction and pipe laying barge. The employing company was North Sea Diving Services, and the fatality date was the 12th of May 1976, the major trauma year for diver deaths in British waters.

On this relatively calm day the wind force was barely 3, with a 9 knot wind blowing a gentle breeze, and the dive was surface orientated, on natural air, into a reasonably comfortable depth of water at 36 metres (120 feet), with an intended surface recompression/decompression following a bottom time of 45 minutes.

The dive was for the purposes of inspection of a construction site using an underwater video camera, and this was apparently successfully completed as the diver commenced a normal ascent consistent with the fact that he was to come straight to the surface chamber. Everything seemed normal to the topside crew, but the diver was unconscious on arrival at the surface. He was immediately transferred to the chamber, with an expert medical team that was on site, and recompressed to depth where attempts were made at resuscitation, but the diver was dead.

It is so amazing that a diver can have so much going for him; air dive, reasonable water depth, surface orientated, obvious communication, no need for water stops, a medical team on site, and yet still lose his life.

This diver died from lung baratrauma/embolism/pneumothorax with a possible collapsed lung, and the diving accident report states that it was possibly caused by too rapid an ascent. On the face of it that would seem a fairly logical conclusion, but once again we ask how could it happen under such ideal conditions?

It was subsequently found that the diving helmet he had used had been poorly maintained, but it was considered that this was not a contributory factor to any reason for the cause and effect.

A Single Buoy Mooring

An SBM is a Single Buoy Mooring (or SPM…a Single Point Mooring) at the end of an oil pipeline and consists of exactly what it says, a huge buoy, perhaps 8-10 metres across on average, floating all alone somewhere offshore of a land-based oil pumping terminal, or an offshore production platform. Tankers conveniently tie up to this buoy to receive oil from one or more pipelines on the seabed, which are connected by one or more large rubber hoses rising from the pipeline end manifold (PLEM) to the underneath of the buoy. The buoy is to support the weight of these hoses that pass through the buoy to loading manifolds on top of the buoy. The buoy also supports the weight of exceptionally large chains, six or more, used to anchor the buoy to the seabed. This is normally accomplished by piling into the seabed at set distances around the buoy and securing the outer ends of the chains to the piles by huge pins or shackles. (Remember our diver whose umbilical was allowed to drift into a boat's stopped propeller? He was working on the end of just such a chain.)

At appointed times the tanker will come up to the buoy and pick up a mooring rope, tie up, and then pick up the loading hoses, connect up, load oil, disconnect and be on its way. Well, it's not quite that straightforward. There has to be communication with the pumping people, and a measurement of the amount of cargo taken on board. All done to clockwork, by *very* skilled operators, but a very expedient way of avoiding harbours and their problems, places where tankers cannot get in, or just plain convenience of operation.

C. DYMOTT

Our next diver died on such an installation in the Irish Sea on the very next day following the death of diver Hubert, on 13th May 1976, though his death would appear not to have been connected with the function or equipment of the SBM itself.

Huge valves on the PLEM need to be opened and closed for loading and maintenance purposes from time to time, and these can be operated remotely or by diver intervention, and though the beneath of the SBM and the hoses down to the PLEM can look somewhat daunting at first sight, it is not an inherently dangerous place to work, though often overshadowed by the buoy, and the water can be gloomy. However, as we have seen, death can strike at a moment's notice in the underwater world, and for no apparent reason, and neither of the two divers on this day suspected that one of them would lose his life.

Diving was for the purpose of debris clearance at the 'SBM Anglesey', working from a supply boat, and the water depth was again at 36 metres. It was to be a daylight dive, with a choppy sea, and a fresh breeze of around Force 5 at 19 knots was blowing. The divers were in SCUBA, on natural air, though not connected to each other. However, one British diver, C.Dymott, who was 26 years old, and with 2-3 years of diving experience, was connected to the surface by a communications line.

As with ascents, a diver should always take his time on a descent too, especially if the surroundings are unfamiliar, but it is reckoned that dropping at 30 metres a minute is not unreasonable. On this occasion however, the divers took five minutes to reach the worksite, an indication that conditions were not particularly good, and they had wisely proceeded with caution.

On arrival at the worksite the second diver apparently became short of air, with a suspected demand valve problem, and signalled to Dymott that he was going back to the surface. Dymott followed him, and was "heard" by the surface to be asking for help. The stand-by diver was deployed and found both divers at the bottom, with Dymott lying on his back on the seabed with his mouthpiece out. The other divers recovered him to the surface, but all attempts at resuscitation did not succeed, and he was officially pronounced dead by the doctor on arrival back at base. Subsequent investigation showed that the diver had drowned, and no real explanation for all that had gone on was forthcoming, though the fatality was categorised as accidental death arising from equipment failure.

The incident duration was said to be ten hours, presumably the time it took for the supply boat to get out to the SBM and to return to base, but the dive duration time was given as *five* hours, for which there appears to be no explanation, nor what kind of equipment was being used for a diver said to be in SCUBA but being "heard" by the surface to be asking for help.

R. DUPUY

This was a French diver about whose fatal dive details in just over 15 metres (51 feet) of water, I have no information whatever except that he was 24 years old and died on the 14th July 1976, on the ETPM 701 (a French installation), in the Central British Sector of the North Sea.

The cause of death was given by pathologist Dr Hendry, at Aberdeen where the body was landed, as cerebral anoxia, a lack of oxygen supply to the brain, caused by equipment design failure.

H.W. SPENSLEY

C.V. MEEHAM

The installation 'Ocean Voyager', a semi-submersible drill rig, was on location in Quadrant 015 of Block 18 in the UK Central Sector of the North Sea on the night of 4th November 1976, when another seemingly innocuous dive session was to take place in a mere ten metres (30 feet) of water, but in bad environmental conditions, with waves washing about at the surface.

The company concerned was K.D. Marine, and the two above divers were to dive in SCUBA, on air, attached to each other with a buddy-line, and to enter the water by basket. Diver Spensley was a British diver of 27 years, and diver Meeham was an American of 24 years of age. The task was one of routine maintenance to "fix a buoy pennant on anchors" and the divers were lowered into the surface of rough water, and left the basket together.

Not long thereafter both divers appeared on the surface holding onto a framework opposite the jobsite, when suddenly Meeham lost his grip on the buddy-line and was washed against columns and drifted away from the rig. A workboat moved in and picked him from the sea.

Well-timed co-ordination is required at the surface to exit the water even in slightly choppy seas, and Spensley was instructed to return to the basket. But he attempted to stand on the slippery surface of an anchor protective cage and was knocked off it by the waves, getting tangled in rope attached to nearby handrails. A manned personnel basket was lowered to his assistance and he was cut free and brought aboard, as was Meeham from the workboat, but they were both dead.

It would appear that both divers had lost their mouthpieces, but it seems certain too, that they may have been knocked unconscious. Once more pathologist Dr Hendry of Aberdeen did his onerous duty and announced that both divers had drowned.

Should these divers have been anywhere near the water under these circumstances? What force motivated them to be doing something so inherently dangerous? As has been said before though, sometimes divers or their supervisors in those yet still early days were driven men, and it was sometimes an intimidating attitude of, "Get on with the job or get on the next boat back", even though operations had been continuing in the North Sea for the best part of ten years, and oil and gas were now on stream. I have seen and experienced these kinds of scenes on many an occasion, and it takes a good man under those circumstances to say he isn't going to get in the water.

After so many years, and as nothing more than an outside observer, not for one moment am I even remotely able to suggest that this was the case on this occasion, but it does make one wonder just what were the whole circumstances that made two otherwise intelligent men risk and lose their lives?

H.R. MOORE

This next British diver, who was 29 years old, was also lost on the surface on a daylight dive, and again in extraordinarily bad seas, seemingly unfit for any kind of sensible diving. The wind was Force 6, a strong breeze, and it was December 24th, proof if proof be needed that work in the business is around the clock, winter or summer, rain or shine, or even on Christmas Eve; and this was the last diver to lose his life in the dreaded year of 1976.

The diving company was yet again Comex, and the platform the Sedneth 701, another semi-submersible drilling rig that was situated in Quadrant 15 of Block 23 in the British Sector of the Central North Sea.

Again two divers were lowered to water level in a basket, and were to dive attached to each other, the object of the exercise being to attach a pennant wire to the crown chain on an anchor. The dive depth was to 20 metres (65 feet), and 12 minutes after entering the water the divers surfaced and the first diver entered the basket. The second diver, Moore, was unable to get into the basket and somehow became disconnected from his buddy diver and drifted away. Although it was daylight he was lost from sight, and seven vessels and a helicopter searched for him to no avail. It was assumed that he had succumbed to exposure and drowned, or had been run down by one of the search vessels as his body was never found.

C.H.HOFFMAN

This next fatality is the only one of its kind ever reported in North European waters, and as far as is known, is the only one of its kind recorded anywhere. The company name is given only as I.U.C.

Divers were in saturation at 150 metres (492 feet) aboard the 'Venture 1', another semi-submersible drill rig, which was stationed in Quadrant 211 of Block 22 of the UK sector of the Northern North Sea. We are now well into 1977, and the accident rate seemed to be improving, but suddenly on May 10th things took a turn for the worse, and yet another diver death occurred.

This was an American diver aged only 22 years, and he was partnered with another diver, 29 year old D.Hammond on an oxy/helium bell run to be employed on apparently routine maintenance work cutting out old or broken wires from posts on the seabed, and fitting new ones.

When the bell was positioned at the worksite, Hoffman left the bell with a 'jacksaw' (presumably a hacksaw) and went to work cutting out two of the wires. He apparently worked very hard at this, and was then told to return to the bell and let his bellman Hammond complete the job. This he did, and Hammond left the bell with new cutting blades, leaving Hoffman inside as his stand-by diver.

After a while, Hoffman reported to the surface that he was feeling very tired, and that the bell oxygen analyser was showing 0.8 instead of 1.4. (Oxygen partial pressure). Communication was then lost between the surface and the bell and Hammond was told to go back to see what the problem was. He found Hoffman in the water beneath the bell and was obliged to reverse the roles and get Hoffman back into the bell.

The total dive and incident took place over four hours and all attempts to recover Hoffman through resuscitation came to nothing. It was concluded that he had fainted "from some unknown cause", and had fallen head first into the bell trunking, where he had drowned.

Pathologist Dr Hendry of Aberdeen was once more in attendance at the post mortem, and it is interesting to note, certainly in the two reports that I have, that no further mention was made of the oxygen analyser.

D. SANSALONE.

On 20th August 1977, this 29-year-old Italian diver was working for Sub Sea Oil Services from the pipe-laying/construction barge 'Semac 1' in Quadrant 14 of Block 7 in the UK Sector of the Central North Sea.

Semac 1 was laying pipe, and we have seen how inherently dangerous this can be for divers, but on this occasion it would appear that the problem was not with the 'stinger', but seemingly with personal equipment failure.

Diving equipment was SCUBA, and the water depth was 23 metres (75 feet), and good visibility was experienced on a daylight dive. Two divers, Sansalone and M. Casadie, *plus* the stand-by diver C. Belluzie, were working on the pipeline stinger, and they were all experienced divers, though not particularly experienced with the hazards and intricacies of pipelaying and stinger diving.

Fifteen minutes into the dive communication was lost with the lead diver Sansalone, though it would appear this communication consisted only of a lifeline, which had parted, or more likely been cut. The lead diver's buddy, Casadie, appeared on the surface, apparently unaware of any problem, and signalled to surface support that air pressure was required on the valve at the stinger site at which the divers were working. The buddy diver then returned to the worksite and, at that time, there was still no sign of or communication with diver Sansalone, so a fourth diver was put into the water to investigate.

Suddenly the buddy diver broke surface to scream out that Sansalone "was dead". The first stand-by diver, Belluzie, having seen Sansalone sinking to the bottom, somehow ran into difficulty himself and surfaced semi-conscious. He was later hospitalised and recovered, but Sansalone's body was recovered from the seabed the following day. His cause of death was given as drowning

R. L. MURPHY.

The above named 26 year old American diver was born on June 22nd 1951 in Denver Colorado, USA, and no reason is given for the fact that, even though he was only in 30 metres of water, according to the HSE report, he was diving surface orientated using an oxy/helium breathing mix.

His employing diving company was Taylor Diving & Salvage Company, Inc., of Louisiana, USA, with a local base in Rotterdam, Netherlands; a big and super efficient company which I was personally associated with in the Middle East, and whom I worked on contract for as a diver and Supervisor, and later along with them in management for another company, over a good many years.

Murphy was working from the 'Trench (or Dredge) Barge 316', property of Brown & Root U.K., in Block K/11 in the Dutch Sector of the North Sea on the late evening of 3rd October 1977, and though the two reports that I have are very brief, being a foreign location, they are also in conflict on the point as to whether or not his umbilical was cut through.

The first report gives the category of the dive as one of a fatality caused by a medical condition, therefore not pressure related. It is stated that there was a loss of communication with the diver, and he was pulled up on his lifeline unconscious. He was put into the decompression chamber where attempts were made to resuscitate him, but no sign of life was observed at any time.

The second report which I have, and which emanates from the same source but was issued two years earlier, states very much the same as the first, but under 'comments' concludes that the diver's umbilical was fouled and his 'pipeline' (umbilical) was cut. It also states that he was yet another diver who did not use his bail out bottle, and died of asphyxia.

However, since researching and producing the above I have received the following from the Staatstoezicht op de Mijnen, the Dutch 'Supervision' of Mines:

"Coordinates of the barge were 53gr, 27' 16,5 N and 3gr, 24' 45E. The barge was working for the Nederlandse Aardolie Maatschappij in Assen.

From investigation it appears that during placing of the Trench machine over a 24" pipeline at a depth of approximately 31 metres all the (diver's) hoses and communication cables were cut at a distance of 2 metres from the diving suit, except for the safety line, which was partly intact."

Diver using 'Kirby Morgan' surface supplied equipment with 'Bale Out' bottle

C. CAILLEUX

This French diver was in fact a Diving Superintendent for Comex Diving, and was born in Algiers on 4 February 1943. His life came to an end at around 1440 hours on 14th October 1977, when he was diving from the Diving Support Vessel 'Talisman' in Block K/14 of the Dutch Continental Shelf. The vessel was working for the Nederlandse Aardolie Maatschappij te Assen, and the work was in 26 metres (85 feet) of water, and seemingly a simple matter, to open a Cameron valve to connect the gas pipeline from the production platform K/14-FA-1 of Nederlande Aardolie Maatschappij to the 36-inch (91.5 cms) gas transport line of Pennzoil.

What a Diving Superintendent was doing making a dive like this is not explained, except that sometimes it's nice to keep your hand in.

"From investigation it appears that the diver started opening the valve when suddenly there was a heavy pressure wave caused by released gas. This gas, at a pressure of 74 bar (over 1000 pounds per square inch) was released at close range through a 2.5 centimetres (one inch) plug (body bleed valve) opening, striking the diver and causing traumatic injury, from which he died.

It was not clear if the plug was not there or was pushed out by the gas."

P. S. AZZOPARDI

Three days after the above diver lost his life, on 17th October, another British diver also lost his life when diving from a Comex saturation unit with a team aboard the 'Zephyr One', a semi-submersible drill rig located in Block 16 of the UK's Western Approaches.

The incident depth was at just under 100 metres (325 feet), and the divers were again said to have been working on non-routine maintenance connected with television equipment. 21 years old Azzopardi, wearing a type 16 Kirby-Morgan band-mask, was out of the bell, and his bellman was a 28-year-old Scandinavian.

Apparently diving had been delayed for several days due to extremely strong tidal conditions, but on this day an attempt was being made to re-connect two guide wires to an underwater base plate. One of the wires had been connected, and the diver was working on the second one when current strength build up coincided with a total loss of communication with him.

Despite the strong current the bellman was deployed, but due to the current strength he could not get to the diver and was obliged to return to the bell. All efforts at signalling and pulling on the diver's umbilical were to no avail, and eventually the bell had to be moved closer to the actual job site before his body, without his helmet on his head, was located and recovered into the bell.

Following a full investigation it was discovered that the locking pin on the diver's helmet was completely missing, and it would appear that movement, tidal current, or some other force had removed the diver's helmet from his head and he had drowned.

Needless to say the categorisation was: "equipment deficiency, leading to personal equipment failure."

D. R. HOOVER

This was the deepest recorded diving fatality to take place in North European waters over the years from 1971 until the end of the 20th Century, and was not necessarily connected with the oilfield business, though it would seem from the report below that it was. But because of its wide interest, and not a little importance, I thought it would not be out of place to include it along with the other divers to whom this overall tribute is directed, and as my own detail is once more scant indeed due to the seeming reluctance of the relevant Norwegian authorities to release years old information, I am indebted to Jackie Warner and his publishers for their permission to extract this from 'Requiem for a Diver'.

"In January, 1978, a diver (an American aged 28 years) lost his life whilst diving in a Norwegian fjord at a depth of 1000 feet (305 metres). He was a member of a team demonstrating underwater welding, to prove that such work could be carried out at such depths.

This was by no means the first time that man had reached the 1000 ft. mark. In simulated and working dives men had gone deeper, but here was a demonstration for the industry of the hardware needed for deeper exploration and development.

The cause of this death has been difficult to establish, although it is possible that the victim was a CO2 (carbon dioxide) retainer…if indeed such a condition exists.

It is more likely that the cause of death was anoxia, due to an interrupted gas supply.

Notwithstanding the fatal accident, the technique of underwater welding at 1000 ft. was demonstrated successfully in UK waters; in fact the surviving members of the original demonstration team remained under pressure (in saturation) at 1000 ft. whilst the diving support vessel steamed to UK waters for the completion of the operation."

The very brief report in my possession contradicts the above cause of death and states under 'Comments': "Possible CO2 poisoning. Starved of gas due to excessive demands from system. Reason for death…asphyxia."

M. WARD

T. PRANGLEY

It will be seen from the date of the next diver deaths that 1978 was an improving year for fatalities as we jump forward to 26th November, when a double tragedy marred what might otherwise have been classed as a 'good' year. Not so for those who lost their lives, of course, and certainly not for their families and friends, but in the face of what had gone before, with 1977 costing so many divers' lives, legislation seemed to be ironing out a good many problem areas where danger lurked, and the vast majority were reaping the benefits. As ever, though, it was taking deaths and accidents to bring about the improvements, and without doubt there are living today very many unwitting survivors.

The daylight of this saturation dive made little difference to the two divers as they descended in the bell, and they personally were barely aware of any problems at the surface even though a Force 8 gale was raging above their heads, once the bell was at the jobsite more than 100 metres (334 feet) beneath the sea. Even if they were aware they would still, perhaps mercifully, have had no conception of the horrible fate that was to befall them within the next three hours.

Their diving company was Nordive, and the dive platform a Diving Support Vessel, the 'Star Canopus' stationed at Beryl Alpha, situated in Quadrant 9 of Block 13 in the UK Sector of the Northern North Sea, and engaged on construction work.

The wind speed had developed to 37 knots, a fresh gale, and the Star Canopus was a DP vessel. In other words, controlled by Dynamic Positioning, without anchors to the seabed and reliant entirely on computer control to operate the vessel's positioning thrusters.

The bell's lead diver Ward, who was 25 years old, and his bellman who was 28, were both experienced British divers, and it was considered that, even though a gale was blowing, with a corresponding sea state, safe, useful work was still within the capability of the vessel, and indeed the divers were still working, with Ward outside the bell. A stage was reached at one time however when Ward came back to the bell, but after a forty-minute period he resumed work again.

One hour and forty-five minutes later the storm was such that the computer 'ran off', the vessel went out of control and off position, and collided with the platform. The dive abort procedure was commenced immediately and Ward went back to the bell, was assisted inside, and the door was closed and dogged down.

Although seas were crashing about, the diving support vessel now came under the control of its main engines, and the bell recovery proceeded to the 30-metre level. Just as it reached that level the bell struck the platform, and lifting was stopped immediately, but the bell wires had caught on an anchor cable and were parted, as were the umbilical and the loadline, the main lifting wire for the bell, and it sank to the seabed with the two divers still inside.

The bell was not located for a further four and a half hours when it was found by searchers using a submersible craft. But it was all too late, and on recovery of the bell both divers were dead, post mortems showing that they died from hypothermia and drowning.

B. EKE

On 5th May 1979, this 34-year-old British diver was working in reasonably comfortable water at just over 31 metres (102 feet), on fixed platform 48/29C, in the UK Sector of the southern gasfields of the North Sea.

It was a daylight dive, but visibility was said to be poor at between one and two metres. The current was mild at half a knot, and with a sea state 1 above, a gentle 9-knot breeze was blowing. Fairly ideal conditions one might say, but how quickly all this can turn to tragedy.

The diver was working for Maritime Offshore Products, surface orientated and therefore tended from the surface, and though no specific personal diving equipment is stated, he was wearing a helmet, and was in communication with the surface. He was using a jet gun on routine maintenance, grit blasting to clean off and inspect 'anodes', which for simplification are huge lumps of a softer than steel metal, connected to the steel of the platform, which erode away instead of the platform.

Some way into the dive, the diver was heard to ask for the jetting equipment to be turned off, followed by further muffled communication, and then nothing. The stand-by diver was immediately deployed into the water, and found the diver with his suit inflated, his helmet off, and apparently drowned. His body was recovered to the surface, but he could not be revived, and the pathologist Dr Calder later confirmed that death was due to drowning.

A subsequent enquiry was again forced to make assumptions when a statement was issued to the effect that it was thought that a slight leak or accidental operation of the suit inflation valve caused the diver's suit to become inflated. Suit inflation is used in dry suits to put a little air into the suit to relieve pinching, especially at the crotch and armpits.

The enquiry report continued that, perhaps on noticing the unwanted extra buoyancy, he tried to disconnect the hose but floated up, becoming entangled in the jet gun, which pulled off his helmet.

Victor GUIEL

Richard WALKER

On the 7th August 1979, these two American divers were in saturation aboard the now famous 'Wildrake', a DSV with dynamic positioning capability, on hire to Infabco Diving Services of Aberdeen, though the vessel was not operating in DP mode at the time of this accident.

The vessel was located way up north at the Thistle Salm Base in Quadrant 211 of Block 19 in the East Shetland Basin, then the UK's most northerly installation in the northern sector of the North Sea, and what followed on this night sent repercussions throughout the whole of the diving industry.

The water depth was in excess of 160 metres (530 feet), and though it was August, the water temperature at that depth, in that location, was icy cold.

Victor Guiel was 29 years old, and Richard Walker was 33, and they were both very experienced gas divers. This night dive into the fatal day of 8th August was for the purpose of reconstructing the pipeline riser and buoy on the Thistle Salm installation, and the divers had been locked off and lowered to working depth in the bell. One of the divers was out of the bell when he noticed that the bell 'loadline', the main lifting wire for the bell, was detached, which meant that the bell was hanging on the umbilical which, of course, was carrying all services to the divers; their gas, communications, and hot water. Not unnaturally the diver reported this, and returned immediately to the bell. He was assisted into the bell, and the bottom door was closed, and the bell was lowered to the seabed to relieve the stress on these services. Communication was bad but, after some time, these were re-established with the bell by means of a through water link, normally tested before every dive as part of the emergency procedure. This however was very bad and served no real purpose.

Divers from a rescue vessel located the lost bell and a recovery wire was secured, but in the attempt to recover the bell the wire also parted, and again the bell was lost more than 120 metres (400 feet) below the surface.

There followed efforts to recover the bell by means of the umbilical, utilising the strengthening wire within the umbilical bundle. This proved to be a disaster, and the umbilical was severed, cutting the divers off completely from all communication and, most importantly, the life preserving hot water system.

The 'Stena Welder' working nearby was brought in to assist, utilising its divers in a rescue bid, but due to "other problems" early attempts were not successful and the bell was not recovered until after 5pm that day.

By the time the bell had been relocated, and yet another wire attached, both divers were found to be dead from the extreme cold, and a later post mortem in Aberdeen confirmed that they had both died from Hypothermia, probably somewhere between the failed early attempts at recovery around noon time, and when they were finally recovered at 5pm.

It is now incumbent on diving contractors that contingency plans should exist for the relocation and recovery of a bell in such circumstances, and the provision of locators.

Much anecdotal evidence was floated around the diving fraternity thereafter, which is quite the norm after an accident or fatality, but it is a reported fact that the split pin holding in the loadline shackle pin had previously been lost, and had been replaced with an improvised split pin - a welding rod. Also there was talk of the bell weight being tied on with rope which therefore could not be released by the divers, and that the 'cowcatcher' type frame which should have been in place at the base of the bell to prevent it sitting right down on the seabed, was not in place, so the divers could not have got out to possibly transfer to another unit anyway. But like I said, the latter two points were but diver gossip, and I have no proof of those myself, though the stories are confirmed in the diving inspector Jackie Warner's book.

In the past, divers have been successfully rescued from such situations by transfer to another bell, and ultimately to another saturation complex, but sadly in this case it was not to be.

This particular case occupied a lot of court time in Scotland where the Crown failed to prove against the accused as employer of the divers, and the civil suits which followed were lengthy and complex, but all we can say about it is that it did all go rather a long way towards improving bell diving operational safety, and more proficient care in the regular inspection and maintenance of such equipment, not least the bell wires, guidance and attaching systems.

The Health and Safety Executive Diving Information Sheet No: 6 dated 2/98 gives major recommendations on this very important matter, though stating quite clearly that nothing within the recommendations is intended to conflict with or set aside any other recommendations, statutory or otherwise, which may relate to the inspection and maintenance of diving bell hoist ropes or associated installations.

D. PHILLIPS

The 29th October 1982, was yet again supposed to be an innocuous day in the life of a diver, but for all the fact that the water depth was shallow, the diver was on natural air, surface orientated and attached to the surface, and the August weather conditions were somewhat benign, this diver still lost his life in a mysterious way, as once again there was no known reason for whatever it was that really took place under the water.

Diver D. Phillips, who was British and 24 years of age, and who, as far as I know, was no relation to the diver J. Phillips who was killed in Scapa Flow in 1974, worked for the diving company Wharton Williams Taylor, otherwise known as 2W. Wharton and Williams were the same two entrepreneurs who, in 1981, were responsible for setting up the operation ending in the ultimate recovery of the gold salvaged from HMS Edinburgh in the Barents Sea, and the Taylor side of things was Taylor Diving & Salvage Company of Belle Chasse, Louisiana, USA.

On 29th October the diving installation was the 'Shearwater Aquamarine', a Diving Support Vessel with a Dynamic Positioning System, which was active on this dive, and the vessel was positioned in the Rough Field in the UK Sector of the Central North Sea.

The water depth was only just over 15 metres (50 feet), and it was a daylight dive, though the underwater visibility was down to 1-2 metres. The surface conditions were sea state two, with half a knot of tide running, and a moderate breeze was blowing at around 14 knots.

The given task was a seabed survey, and this ex-Royal Navy ship's diver was well qualified for the job in hand having received civilian training at Fort Bovisand in Devon, in addition to his Navy training.

He was working on the seabed when there was a sudden failure of the computer controlling the vessel's Dynamic Positioning System, and the diver was dragged off the job by the out of control vessel, and "who then bailed out from his KB17 (Kirby Morgan) helmet." The stand-by diver was deployed but no sign of the diver was found, even though he was equipped with an emergency bail out air supply.

Apparently no alarms went off on the DP vessel, and the system checked out OK, though it was suspected that there was some mistake made by the bridge officers, but there was no indication of criminal negligence or breach of legislation and therefore no prosecution followed.

The Coroner's inquest returned an open verdict, as at 18th April 1983 the body of the diver had not been recovered. However, in another report in my possession, though the reason for death was given as not known, it does state: 'Body not recovered until months later. Suspected equipment was slipped.'

Jarle PEDERSEN

Jarle was a Norwegian diver aged 29 years who lost his life in the Norwegian sector of the North Sea on 16th March 1983, when his umbilical, and subsequently Jarle himself, was drawn into one of the 'thrusters' on a vessel operating in Dynamic Positioning mode. The working water depth was just seven metres.

At 3pm in the afternoon of that day it was reported to the Norwegian Oil Directorate by a member of Phillips Petroleum Company, Norway, that a diver had disappeared whilst diving from a vessel, the 'Seaway Falcon' described as a 'Flex reel/Rigid j-lay ship'.

It transpired that the vessel had been instructed to move to a new workplace at '2/4T' in the Ekofisk Field to carry out work on the 'Ekofisk tank's north side'. A vessel I have not been able to find any information on, but in any event the 'Seaway Falcon' was instructed to moor up beside it for the necessary diving work to be carried out, but was unable to do so, not finding suitable mooring points. It was decided therefore to moor up at riser platform 2/4R, 20 metres away, from where it would apparently not be difficult to reach the worksite at 2/4T.

It was normal for the 'Seaway Falcon' to moor with one hawser forward and one aft, and then activate the aft thrusters on constant thrust, pushing the vessel away from the platform, whilst the forward thruster was placed under the control of the Gyro Compass, thus holding the vessel in a fixed position. When all was ready it was announced from the bridge to the diving supervisor that diving could begin.

Jarle Pedersen, the diver, was made aware of what work had to be done, and also of the discharge of cooling water from the tank 2/4T which could create 'whirlpool currents' and make work difficult. He was asked to check to see if the work was feasible from that position, by swimming on the surface outside of the discharge area. He entered the water by means of a basket, took the end of the downline, and swam to the workplace as instructed, securing the downline on arrival. He reported that it was completely possible to carry out the work despite the discharge, and commenced work with a wire brush and scraper, cleaning off seagrowth.

After some time he asked for the hydraulic powered steel brush to be sent down but as the work was only at seven metres, the angle of the downline was too shallow for the tool to be run down it to him and he was asked to come back along the downline to pick it up. The diver reported he was on his way, but also that the current was increasing in strength. The dive supervisor told him to come back to the basket and asked him where his umbilical was, but was told by the diver that he did not know exactly due to poor visibility. The deck crew were told to pick up on the diver's hose, but almost immediately this was found to be snagged up somewhere, but the diver reported being back in the basket. The supervisor again asked where his umbilical was leading, and the diver reported it was to the stern.

The supervisor was then about to call up the bridge for the thrusters to be stopped, but before he was able to do so the diver cried out three times, "Stop the thrusters". They were the last words he ever spoke.

On getting through to the bridge, the supervisor was told that the thrusters were stopped, someone having run to the bridge, as just prior to the supervisor's call the diver's hose was ripped from the hands of the tender, who knew immediately what had happened.

The stand-by diver was in the water within one minute, just as the first diver's hose came bubbling to the surface. The stand-by could not find the diver at that time, but his body was recovered the following day.

It would seem that a combination of current and cooling water had carried a bight of the diver's slack hose into the thrusters's blades as he returned to the basket, with fatal consequences.

Note: I refer the reader to the case of Bradley Westell (Page 172) who was also drawn into a vessel's thrusters, and the HSE recommendation notes at the end of that case report.

R. M. WALLACE

Again here we have what looks like a straightforward piece of diving work, but again it turned to tragedy for no known reason.

It was 2nd June 1983, and the diver, who was 30 years old, was working at fixed platform 8A in the UK's North Sea Central Sector for Mobell (Marine), from the diving installation 'Mobell Diver', but operating from a small inflatable in a little more than 16 metres (54 feet) of water. He was well enough experienced for the job he was doing, having attended a diving course at one of the well known diving schools in the UK, and had been diving professionally for about two years.

The weather was again calm on this daylight dive, with little wind or tide, but the underwater visibility at $1-2$ metres was once more poor for the time of year and location.

In this depth the diver was breathing normal air from SCUBA, and was inspecting a pipeline from the beach to a platform, free diving, but with a line from him attached to a small buoy at the surface. This was to be a no decompression dive, which would give about one hour at this depth on most dive tables.

When the diver was signalled to come up there was no reply, and no movement, so the stand-by diver was deployed who found and recovered the diver's apparently lifeless body with his mouthpiece out. At no time was any sign of life seen in the diver, and resuscitation was ineffective. The report states that it is not known how long the diver had been unconscious on the bottom as no indication whatever was given that there was any problem, and he was wearing a lifejacket.

It was later declared that he had died from saltwater drowning.

William CRAMMOND-32 years- British
Edwin COWARD-35 years-British
Roy LUCAS-38 years-British
B.BERGERSEN-29 years-Norwegian
T.HELLEVICK-34 years-Norwegian

Four of the above divers were in saturation and died horrendously in one terrible moment in the early morning of 5th November, 1983, aboard the drilling rig 'Byford Dolphin' which was being worked by Elf Aquitaine Norge A/S at well 25/7-B5 in the North East Frigg Field in the Norwegian Sector of the North Sea. As a direct result of the accident William Crammond, who was employed by Comex Haulder Diving Limited and was acting as a surface support operator, also died shortly thereafter, and a further surface support operator, Mr Saunders, was seriously injured. All of the six men, in fact, were working for the French diving company Comex.

It would appear that diving work was progressing satisfactorily on the wells when it was reported that bad weather was expected. The diving bell was brought to the surface and clamped to the deck decompression chamber. During the transfer of divers from the bell to the DDC, there was a sudden and catastrophic uncontrolled explosive decompression of the whole complex when the clamp between the chamber and the bell suddenly released, killing the four divers within the system, two British and two Norwegian, and severely injuring the two British surface support divers outside the complex, one of whom – William Crammond – who had been working on the clamp, could not be found in the aftermath of the explosion. A search was instituted and Mr Crammond was found, severely injured, aboard the 'Byford Dolphin'. The stand-by boat, along with two other supply boats, had searched the immediate sea area, and the stand-by boat reported finding 'a green helmet' at sea. Everyone having been accounted for by that time, the sea search was called off.

Immediately after the accident the 'Byford Dolphin' captain and the Elf Aquitaine superintendent went to the diving unit. Upon confirming the need for hospital treatment, the radio room was asked to inform the North East Frigg-Field Control Station to request immediate helicopter transport from Frigg for injured persons

The two injured divers were air lifted out by helicopter for Rogaland Hospital, Stavanger with an ETA there of 0647, but it was too late for Mr Crammond who died in the helicopter.

At around 0900 a helicopter arrived from shore with representatives from the Police, Comex, EAN, and the Norwegian Petroleum Directorate, when an immediate investigation into the circumstances of the accident was instituted.

The bodies of the four dead divers were later flown ashore on the same helicopter to Gades Institute in Bergen, and by 1600 hours that day the rig was released by the Police and the NPD, and all Comex personnel involved in the accident were evacuated ashore.

The saturation system had been pressurised to a depth of 100 metres, apparently with all internal doors open, when the bell suddenly became detached from the complex as described in Chapter 8, and all divers died almost instantaneously from 'explosive decompression', as the description implies, a rapid, uncontrolled decompression. When this occurs during a saturation dive the very rapid expansion of gas within the lungs, plus the massive and rapid release of dissolved gas from within the body tissues, will result in extensive tissue damage. It is believed that one of the divers on this day was forced through the part open hatch. No way to die can be a good way, except in your sleep perhaps, but these divers in the last seconds of their lives knew what was happening to them, and this must have been truly horrendous.

In their Diving Information Sheet No: 4 dated 9/98, the HSE has endorsed a safety notice issued by the Norwegian Petroleum Directorate in connection with diving accidents on the Norwegian Shelf. Briefly, it recommends that clamping mechanisms necessary for a chamber complex evacuation device and bell to remain under pressure should be fitted with an interlocking mechanism to make it impossible to open a clamping mechanism in the event that an undesirable drop in pressure will take place, with emphasis that it must be impossible to open the mating clamp between the bell and the chamber whilst the tunnel (which connects the two) is under pressure.

In addition, ACOP 71, with respect to the requirements of the Diving at Work Regulations 1997, under the heading Transfer under Pressure, now points out the risk of the possibility of catastrophic depressurisation when divers or equipment are being transferred into or out of a saturation chamber and states, "Internal doors, that is those between the transfer chamber and the trunking to the diving bell, and those separating living chambers within the chamber complex, should be kept closed at all times except when divers are passing through them."

So we know in detail *what* happened, but the main point is why? I am afraid I have not been given access to this information, but once again we can all, hopefully, draw solace from the safety recommendations that came forth from this terrible accident.

I do know however that one of the lectures for divers on Life Support Technicians courses at one of the diver training schools covers the structure and main points of Norwegian legislation as it applies to chamber and bell operations. In addition, the schools Closed Bell Syllabus deals very closely with Transfer Under Pressure Procedures, which is said to be, as is obvious, a very dangerous time during a saturation dive.

**Deck of 250 tonne Crane Barge
with Saturation System in rear container**

M. DAWSON

On 15th August 1984, this 22 year old British diver was working from the Diving Support Vessel 'Deurloo', in the Leman Field, and his employing company was the world renowned and well-respected international diving company, Oceaneering. The location was quadrant 049 of block 27 of the UK's southern North Sea gasfields, and the water depth was 43 metres (140 feet).

Again this was a surface orientated daylight dive, and on this one I would agree that it was the kind of accident that could happen to anyone, as when working with hydraulic tools we are talking about lots of torque, ever ready to rip right out of your hands.

No diving equipment type is discussed, but it is known that the diver was working with surface supplied natural air, and was in communication with the surface.

The diver had two to three years of diving experience, and seemed well suited to the demands of the job in hand, which was a non-routine maintenance drilling operation, using a hydraulic drill, on a lower brace of an unidentified structure. Suddenly all communication ceased and the stand-by diver went into the water, only to find diver Dawson lying on the bottom with his helmet off. For reasons not given, but it is assumed he was wrapped up in the drill and hydraulic hose, the stand-by diver was unable to recover the apparently lifeless body of the diver to the surface, and neither could a second stand-by diver!

By this time a strong tidal flow was picking up, and it was decided to abort any further diving operations until the next slack water. At that time the diver's body was recovered with some difficulty after the release of a 'clog clamp', and it was noticed that he had suffered bruising and lacerations.

It would appear that his Heliox-18 band mask had been removed from his head by a bight of rope formed by tangling with the powerful rotation of the drill bit, and the inquest verdict was that he had died an accidental death from asphyxia caused by saltwater drowning.

William (Bill) CARR

This was another very experienced offshore British diver, with fourteen years in the business, who lost his life in the North Sea under totally unnecessary circumstances and, to this day, his family is not satisfied that the subsequent enquiry following his death through grossly violated work conditions sufficiently pursued every possibility to bring the case to a satisfactory conclusion in taking care of a young widow and two small children left to face the world without a loving husband and father.

Bill, or Billy, as he was known, lived in Warrington, Cheshire, and was a fit and very healthy man who had worked on rigs off Scotland, Scandinavia, and on the Ivory Coast. In February 1987 he took a diving refresher course in Denmark due to changing regulations, and following successful completion started work with Comex Diver Holdings Ltd on 1st March 1987.

On 17th March 1987, 38 years old Bill, the husband of Anne, and father to young Billy aged 10, and his sister Suzanne aged 6, left home to go to work under the Norwegian North Sea, and was never seen alive by his family again.

During the evening of March 30th he was working from the 'Seaway Condor', a Flexible reel-lay ship, stationed in the Oseberg Field. Norsk Hydro and Norcem Comex were the operator and the diving contractor respectively, and the hired diving vessel and crew were Stolt-Nilsen Norway. He was out of a bell at 110 metres (360 feet) operating a mud-dredging machine, being tended by his bellman, diver M.Sullivan.

This second of the current bell-run dive had commenced at 1839 hours and, previous to the first dive, both divers had checked the equipment to be used, and though a little concerned about a loose securing bolt on the Kirby-Morgan Superlite 17 helmet, Sullivan, who was the first diver out, tended by Bill, considered that "nothing was seriously wrong" with the equipment. He *was* concerned, however, at being told by the supervisor to close **both** valves on the Bail-Out system, as the system leaked. Unbelievably, this conversation seems to have been carried no further. It transpired however that Sullivan, during his dive, found the contents of his emergency supply seriously depleted and a fresh set was sent down to him. He also experienced a lack of hot water going through his suit and at one stage had to return to the bell.

Following the change-round, on which Bill used the same equipment as Sullivan, some forty minutes into his dive, Bill complained that he was not getting any gas and asked that he be pulled back to the bell. Previous to this, Sullivan had noticed a large amount of water in the water trap of the gas reclaim system, an indication of excess water in the diver's helmet. Sullivan was about to mention this both to Bill and the surface supervisor, when Bill had complained of a lack of gas. It would appear that both the bellman and the surface supervisor understood what was said and moves were made to resolve the problem. Shortly after the last conversation, communication was lost with the diver, though the supervisor still advised him to use his reserve gas. This was impossible for the diver, as shown below.

On the basis of tape-recordings it was later assumed that at that point he had lost his helmet. When the body was finally recovered to the surface chamber, after heart massage and mouth-to-mouth resuscitation had been carried out in transit, and in the chamber, a doctor was finally locked into the chamber and pronounced Bill dead at 2338 hours.

The report of the Norwegian Petroleum Directorate states that, on the basis of the recordings, the diving supervisor was not concentrating sufficiently on the diver in the water. In the control room things were being discussed that had nothing to do with the work that was being carried out. The bellman, who apparently had had no training in how to get an unconscious diver into a bell, reported that he could not pull the diver back to the bell, and a whole catalogue of serious acts and omissions then began to unfold.

The bellman was instructed to leave the bell to recover the diver, which took six minutes, mostly due to the inefficiency of the hot water system. It was later discovered that he had not set up the emergency hoisting equipment correctly, nor had he followed correctly other necessary procedures. A second bell had to be launched with divers to assist getting Bill into the first bell, which had a very narrow (630mm) trunking, though Sullivan, with difficulty, *had* got Bill's head out of the water into a gas atmosphere and had commenced mouth-to-mouth resuscitation.

The valve to allow flooding of the bell to a degree to allow any casualty to be more easily floated into the bell was missing. The surface TV monitor for the bell interior was out of order so that the surface supervisor could not see what was going on. Surface help was slow in forthcoming in launching the No: 2 bell to assist in the recovery. The valves on the diver's Bail-Out system, one on the helmet and one on the bottle, were *both* closed, when the one on the bottle should have been open, leaving the diver enabled to operate his own helmet valve in an emergency. There had been several problems with the hot-water system prior to this occasion. There had not been sufficient training in how to recover an unconscious diver into a bell, the duty supervisor stating that there had been no such training before they were mobilised. The log for the maintenance of the diving helmets showed that there had been several cases of the locking mechanism bending. The assistant supervisor was not in his correct place in the dive control room. There also appears to have been some confusion as to which company's emergency procedure should be used, and there was no checklist for the diver's personal equipment in use, Bill having no separate harness, his umbilical being connected to his Bail-Out harness.

The subsequent investigation by the Norwegian Petroleum Directorate and the Police concluded that the accident was caused by a failure of the mechanism that holds the helmet onto the diver's neck seal, with the result that the diver lost his helmet. The 'Preliminary Conclusion' of the committee of the personnel involved, conducted on the 1st April 1987, was that "The accident was due to a progressive loss of seal between the clamp/neck dam arrangement and the shell of the diving helmet."

Following this, Diving Safety Memorandum No: 3/1987, was put out by R.Giles, the then Chief Inspector of Diving at the UK Department of Energy which at that time had responsibility for diving, as previously mentioned, pointing out "The importance of well maintained and functional main locking mechanisms and locking systems" on diving helmets. Did the supposedly highly professional and well trained and versed diving companies, managers, superintendents, supervisors and divers really need to be told this?

There are at least another sixteen pages to this report involving the possibility of infringements by the various companies involved, and in my opinion it is absolutely appalling that no criminal prosecution of any kind or any person within any of the companies was recommended. All infringements were categorised as, "not comprising a serious disregard of the safety regulations", even though the Health and Safety at Work etc Act 1974 applies to all persons at work whether employers, employees or the self-employed. (See 'Changes in Diving Regulations. p184).

Once again it took the death of a good man to prompt changes, to close the door after the horse was gone, and the Safety Manager of the diving contracting company Norcem Comex Subsea (NCS) put out a memo to all diving personnel that the company had implemented a safety pin to lock the lever on the neckdam of the diving helmets, and had been in touch with the helmet manufacturers in regard to reinforcing the locking lever to prevent bending.

On a personal note, both Bill and Anne's children have been wonderfully raised by their mother's unselfish efforts over the last fifteen years, and received University education. Anne, who lost "the love of her life", has never re-married, and still lives in the family home.

There is only one commendable thing to have come out of this family's painful loss, and that is that the death of their loved one, without a doubt, saved the lives of others.

Bradley WESTELL

At this juncture we arrive at 1995 with this wonderful and extraordinary jump in time, there having been no diver fatalities whatever in the North Sea since 1987, and no British diver had lost his life there since 1984. But unfortunately the respite was not to last, and this British diver lost his life on 31st July, 1995, when working in shallow saturation from the Diving Support Vessel 'Stena Orelia.'

But he was not to die by some act or omission on his own part, lack of proper training or experience, inadequate equipment, nor in any kind of mysterious circumstances, but by admitted neglect on the part of the employing company responsible for the diver's safety in terms of the Health and Safety at Work Act 1974, who were tried and convicted at Norwich Crown Court. Also, the Dive Supervisor who had supervised the bell run and locked out the diver, and who had just been relieved on watch before the incident, pleaded not guilty when charged with his manslaughter and was found not guilty on that charge, but guilty of Perverting the Course of Justice and was sentenced to a term in prison.

Bradley Westell was 29 years old and was a top class bell diver with various diving qualifications to his credit. He had around 8 years of diving experience, and on the day of his death was working in Quadrant 48 of Block 19 in the UK's Southern Sector of the North Sea. This was a night dive, and a classic example of a disaster arising because a diver was extended too far out on his umbilical, especially at night, and especially working in the vicinity of the thrusters of an operating Dynamic Positioned vessel.

The task was in 25 metres (82 feet) of water, and consisted of monitoring the laying of a power cable from the 'Stena Orelia'. The diver became extended to the full 65 metres (213 feet) length of his umbilical where he was endeavouring to sort out a problem, and then returned to his original position and continued to monitor the power cable.

At the end of the dive Bradley was returning to the bell when suddenly all communication was lost when the slack in his umbilical was drawn up into one of the vessel's thrusters. He too was then pulled into the thrashing blades where massive traumatic injury killed him instantly. His body was later recovered on the surface.

At the Norwich Crown Court on 14th January 1997, the guilty company was tried and upon its own admission was convicted upon indictment of:
Failing to take adequate precautions
Failing to ensure the health and safety at work of its employees

and on 23rd July 1997 was sentenced to be:

Fined on one count under Section 2 of the Health and Safety at Work Act 1974, and one count under the Diving Operations at Work Regulations, Regulation 12 (3), and was fined £100,000 on each count, with £25,000 to be paid towards the costs of the prosecution.

At the same Court on 30th June 1997, the dive supervisor, who had pleaded not guilty on both counts, was found not guilty of manslaughter, but was tried and was convicted upon indictment of:
Doing an act tending and intended to pervert the course of public justice. (This was in connection with video taped records relating to the dive.)
Failing to take reasonable care for the safety of another, namely Bradley Westell

and on 23rd July 1997 was sentenced to:

On the first count, one month imprisonment, and on the second count fined £500, or in default to serve 14 days imprisonment consecutive to count one.

It should be noted that the Certificates of Conviction issued to me on 29.3.2000 in respect to the above are subject to any appeal against conviction of which notice, or notice of application for leave to appeal, has been or may be given, under the Criminal Appeal Act 1968.

The Health and Safety information sheet No.1 dated 2/98 makes certain recommendations concerning diving work undertaken from Dynamically Positioned vessels, one of the most important of which is the need for close supervision of the diver, good diver tending, and comprehensive communication coverage at all times.

All pretty obvious you might say, but it is very easy to get carried away on some diving jobs, especially in shallow water, with the idea that nothing can go wrong because it seems straightforward enough, and it's all been done before. But it just cannot be stressed strongly enough how important it is to be mentally aware at all times whilst such a potentially dangerous job is in progress of exactly what is going on from moment to moment, and to be doubly aware on extra hazardous work of exactly what could go wrong at any one of those given moments. That way you are ahead of the game and not wise after the event.

In précis, in pointing out that diving from DP vessels in operational mode is particularly hazardous for obvious reasons, and that Diving Contractors should ensure that each diving operation is carried out from a suitable safe place, this is what the HSE Diving Information Sheet has to say on the subject:

"Vessels must be operated in such manner that all statutory requirements are met, and that all personnel used on such operations should have the necessary skills to undertake such operations safely, and that Diving Rules must incorporate proper procedures which emphasise the importance of close and efficient supervision, good diver tending and comprehensive communications between surface control and the diver at all times."

And last but certainly by no means least, "if a safe diving position cannot be maintained, then diving should not take place."

Gary A. CAREY

The penultimate diver death in the North Sea culminated in the prosecution and conviction of two companies, Cooper Cameron (UK) Limited, and Mobil North Sea Limited, both under Section 3 of the Health & Safety at Work Act 1974. They were charged with being employers in terms of the above Act, and failing to conduct an undertaking in such a way as to ensure so far as was reasonably practicable that persons *not* in their employment who may be affected thereby were not exposed to risks to their health or safety.

Gary Carey, a 38 year old British diver from Okehampton in Devon, was employed by Subsea International Offshore of Aberdeen, and was working from the Diving Support/Flex-lay ship 'Discovery' in the UK's Northern Sector of the North Sea. The work to hand was at the installation wellhead 9/13b-38z in the Ness subsea template near the installation Beryl 'B' in position Latitude 59 degrees 33 minutes 37.032 seconds North, and Longitude 01 degree 25 minutes 52.233 seconds East, an area designated by Order in Council under Section 1 (7) of the Continental Shelf Act 1964. (See later note).

On 11th August 1996 the divers left the saturation complex for a 'routine maintenance' night bell dive to 100 metres, with fair underwater visibility of about 3 metres. Surface conditions were calm, though irrelevant to the divers at that depth, and the tide was running at just half a knot, with a seawater temperature of around 5 degrees C.

Two divers were being tended out of the bell and the lead diver Gary, who was a top class bell diver, was accompanied by another diver, Roland Brumley, of whom, I am sorry to say, I know only his name. Their task was to remove a wellhead pressure cap from a 'Christmas Tree' using a power wrench. In the process of doing so there was an explosion and the cap blew off under high pressure, crushing and severely injuring Gary in the thigh and pelvic area, and injuring Roland Brumley.

Although divers are specifically trained in the rescue and care of an injured diver, the task is by no means an easy one, and there was apparently great difficulty in getting the divers back into the bell, especially as Gary was unconscious, but recovery to the surface complex was achieved where both divers received expert medical aid on site, and by way of onshore communication, but Gary died in the chamber.

One of the charges brought against Cooper Cameron was that a system of work was planned for the replacement of a shear pin on the annulus master valve on the Christmas Tree at the wellhead, without the provision of two mechanical pressure barriers being placed in position below the master valve to prevent the flow of wellhead liquids through to the master valve and surrounding area, thus placing all personnel not employed by the accused in that area at risk to their health and safety.

The charges against Mobil North Sea Limited were more complex involving failure to ensure that: the well history was properly maintained so that all relevant information relating to the condition of the well was properly recorded; the adoption of a proper Hazard Identification procedure; proper Risk Assessment, and most importantly, that a detailed and comprehensive Pre-Workover Procedure was effected so that persons required to release pressure from the void space below the pressure cap, which was essential for the safe removal of the cap, were made fully aware of safe methods of assessing the state of pressure within the void space and releasing the pressure.

At Aberdeen Sheriff court on 2nd March 1998, Mobil North Sea Ltd were found guilty on one charge under Section 3 of the Health and Safety at Work Act 1974, and were fined £175,000.

At the same Court on the same day Cooper Cameron Ltd were found guilty on one charge under Section 3 of the same Act and were fined £45,000.

Current Legal Requirement

Whenever diving operations are planned and conducted on the United Kingdom Continental Shelf there are several sets of regulations that must be consulted and applied such as:

The Health and Safety at Work etc. Act 1974 - Chapter 37.

An Act to make further provisions for securing the health, safety and welfare of persons at work, for protecting others against risks to health or safety in connection with the activities of persons at work...

A Christmas Tree

A so called 'Christmas Tree' is a submarine wellhead, an assembly of well operating valves which gets its name from the fact that it looks like a tree, with branches of pipes and valves sticking out all around it. The device fits over a wellhead if it is to be completed as a subsea system; needless to say that is one beneath the water, on the seabed, rather than a structure which projects above the water, and contains the connections necessary for the coupling up to it of various production flowlines to take the oil ashore.

Christopher HILL

Christopher, who was married with a family, was the very last commercial diver to die in the 20th Century whilst engaged on the exploitation of oil or gas from the British Sector of the North Sea. From the official report he was employed on construction work, was British, and 42 years old, and was killed on the 6th August 1999, in the north-west corner of the Forties Field at Buchan Alpha, on what is known as the Buchan Template, in Quadrant 21, Block 1A, whilst working for Stolt Comex Seaway Limited from the Diving Support Vessel 'Discovery'.

He was by all accounts an excellent diver, HSE certificated, and, according to the press, with more than 20 years of commercial experience. He was diving from a saturation bell in 117 metres (383 feet) of water. Whilst engaged there on a cutting operation using subsea burning equipment, there was an apparent accumulation of cutting gases (hydrogen and oxygen) or of hydrocarbon products in an overhead space or void, resulting in an underwater explosion from which the diver suffered traumatic injury, and his helmet was blown off. The dive supervisor saw the incident on a TV monitor and called to the diver several times, without reply. Although on recovery resuscitation was carried out, and expert medical aid was immediately available on site, it would appear that he was killed instantly.

This was a daylight dive on a calm day, though at that depth this would have made little difference to the divers. A light half to one knot tide was running, and a second diver with Chris, 40 year old John Dodds, who was/ is also an HSE certificated bell diver with many years of experience, was blown back by the explosion, but managed to drag Chris back to the bell where bellman Adam Blackden assisted the divers into the bell. From the official report it would appear that neither diver Dodds nor Blackden have since returned to work.

Although responsibility under the Health and Safety at Work Act was initially denied by Stolt Offshore, they later pleaded guilty to an amended charge of failing to ensure the health and safety of employees, and of failing to provide a safe system of work, and were fined £60,000 at Aberdeen city's Sheriff Court. Fiscal deputy Andrew Grant said that this was not a freak accident, and little consideration had been given to reducing the risk of explosion. The company concerned had failed to carry out a satisfactory risk assessment and hazard identification related to the work, resulting in this tragic fatality.

Stolt's legal defence John Mitchell said that the company deeply regretted the tragic accident, and that following a detailed investigation by the company into the explosion, a safety notice was issued regarding procedures to ensure, so far as "humanly possible", that there would be no possible repeat of such an accident.

Chris Hill was the 58th and last diver to die between 1971 and 1999, and was the 38th British diver to lose his life in that period in giving their all in playing their very important and vital part in the extraction of our oil and gas resources.

Changes in Diving Regulations

In 1964 the United Kingdom Continental Shelf Act vested in her Majesty the Queen of England any rights exercisable by the United Kingdom outside territorial waters with respect to the seabed and subsoil and the natural resources.

This Act provided that the licensing arrangements applicable onshore (to hydrocarbon resources) in Great Britain, would be extended offshore and should include provision for "the safety, health and welfare of persons employed on operations undertaken with the authority of the licensee" i.e. civil and criminal law of England, Scotland and Northern Ireland, and certain statutory laws expressly provided for application in these areas.

This Act formed the basis of regulatory powers in the early important phase of development of the offshore industry. As the exploration and development proceeded, more specific legislation was required. The Minerals Working (Offshore Installation) Act 1971 was passed which enabled the Secretary of State for Energy to make regulations to cover other facets of operations.

The first regulations relating to diving operations were those made in 1960 by the Minister of Labour for Factories Act purposes (Special Diving Operations) SI 688.

In 1974, the Offshore Installations (Diving Regulations) SI 1229 came into force. This was necessary because of the new developments in diving technology that enabled men to work at much greater depths and for longer periods of time using saturation diving techniques. These regulations considerably expanded the scope of supervision of men working in deeper and more hazardous waters.

In 1975, the Merchant Shipping (Diving Operations) Regulations, SI 116 came into operation. These regulations were applied to all diving operations from UK ships anywhere outside UK territorial waters, except those activities on the UK Continental Shelf coming within the scope of the Diving Operations at Work Regulations 1981.

In 1976, the Secretary of State for Energy made further regulations in respect of submarine pipelines and associated works. The Submarine Pipelines (Diving Operations) Regulations 1976 SI 923; although to all intents and purposes these regulations were identical, did not apply to diving operations covered by the 1974 regulations, nor to the regulations made in 1975 for the merchant shipping diving operations.

In 1977, the order in council extended the powers of the Health and Safety at Work Act 1974 to cover those engaged in the offshore oil and gas industry. On 28 May 1989, the Health and Safety at Work etc Act 1974 (Application outside Great Britain) Order 1989 SI 840 came into force, revoking the 1977 order in council.

The 1989 order in council also encompasses those engaged in construction work, loading and unloading ships, shipbuilding and repairing and diving operations in territorial waters. The 1974 Act applies to all persons at work whether employers, employees or self-employed. Employers are required to ensure the safety of their employees by ensuring adequate instruction, training and supervision as well as maintaining safe plant, work systems and premises. This comprehensive Act considerably increased the responsibilities of everyone working in the offshore industry.

In 1978, a Government working party, which looked into the problems of diving safety, reported that a single set of regulations was most practical and desirable and that it should cover all diving at work operations carried out inside Great Britain, in territorial waters or on the Continental Shelf.

In 1981, after liaison between the HSE Safety Executive and the Department of Energy, the Secretary of State for Employment made the 1981 Diving Operations at Work Regulations under the 1974 Health and Safety at Work Act. The 1981 Regulations applied in Great Britain and offshore. These Regulations have the object of simplifying, and making more uniform, the legislation relating to everyone "diving for gain". They revoked the Diving Operation Regulations of 1960 and the Offshore Installations (Diving Operations) Regulations 1974, and have priority over those of the Merchant Shipping Act of 1975. The 1976 Submarine Pipeline (Diving Operations) Regulations were however not revoked at the time, but were revoked in August 1993.

As previously mentioned, in 1991, following the publication of the Cullen Report into the Piper Alpha disaster which killed 167 men, the Government accepted all 126 recommendations made in the Report and transferred all the enforcement sections in the Department of Energy, Petroleum Engineering Division, to the newly formed Offshore Safety Division of the HSE. This transfer ended a rather unique arrangement whereby a licensing authority, the Department of Energy, also held the responsibility for the safety and well being of the workforce employed in that industry.

In 1992, all legislation made under the Mineral Working Act of 1971 was, by Act of Parliament, made Relevant Statutory Provisions under the Health and Safety at Work etc. Act, thereby officially transferring all legislative and enforcement responsibilities to the newly formed Offshore Safety Division.

On 1st April 1998, the current Diving at Work Regulations 1997 came into force revoking the Diving Operations at Work Regulations 1981 and amendments of 1990 and 1992.

On 10th December 1997, under the Health and Safety at Work etc Act 1974, and also coming into force on 1st April 1998, a Code of Practice entitled 'Commercial diving projects offshore' was consented to by the Secretary of State, and approved by the Health and Safety Commission, "for the purposes of providing practical guidance with respect to the Diving at Work Regulations 1997."

Health and Safety - the Future

The chairman of the International Marine Contractors Association in a recent statement when talking of how IMCA "works to ensure that its guidelines are accepted as reliable and comprehensive standards to which all project personnel can work in a competent and safe manner", referred to how in the North Sea IMCA works actively with the Cross Industry Safety Leadership Forum's 'Step Change Support Group' to ensure IMCA guidelines both support and reflect the goals of the Health, Safety and Environmental Performance Improvement Initiatives for the UK offshore industry.

During the past year, a cross industry safety forum has been developing an initiative aimed at further improving safety performance in the UK offshore industry, and represented on this forum are The UK Offshore Operators Association Limited, the International Association of Drilling Contractors (North Sea Chapter), and the Offshore Contractors Association, who have joined forces in producing a commitment statement headed: 'A Step Change In Safety - It's Our Business.'

They have kindly given me permission to reproduce the following:

"During recent years, safety in our oil and gas industry has improved significantly. Dedication and hard work by everyone involved in the industry have reduced the numbers of serious incidents that occur. Our safety record is now better than in many industries that work in equally challenging environments.

Encouraged by what has been achieved so far, we remain committed to further improvements in our safety performance. Such progress is possible but will require a fundamental change in attitude by everyone, and greater co-operation across our industry.

This must start with leadership. Therefore we declare our personal commitment to action in three key areas.

We will:

Deliver a 50% improvement in the whole industry's performance over the next 3 years.

Establish our own safety performance contracts that will demonstrate visibly our personal concern for safety as an equal to business performance.

Work together to improve sharing of safety information and good practice across the whole industry, through active involvement of employees, service companies, operators, trades unions, regulators and representative bodies.

As we lead our industry into the next millennium, we ask you to join us in creating a new environment in which cross industry collaboration will help to place safety at the top of everyone's personal agenda."

Because I haven't personally been involved in the offshore industry for a very long time, when I read the kind of publication from which the above was extracted, and look through the pages of other relevant publications, I can scarcely believe the changes that have taken place in the last thirty years and, recognising that, yes, it's a long time, it still seems barely credible to me how those utterly and totally committed persons and organisations over the years have changed the face of the offshore industry's safety record, practically beyond all recognition, through safe working practices based on high level training initiatives which have been so instrumental in personnel at all levels developing such a powerful and dedicated safety culture.

There is absolutely no doubt whatsoever, that those divers who lost their lives in the North Sea oil and gas industry over the last three decades were indirectly responsible in many ways for preserving the lives of numbers of divers living today, and divers of the future, and for that I sincerely hope that this book will go a long way towards ensuring that they will never be forgotten.

Unions

Historically, and briefly, the Association of British Professional Divers was founded in London in 1974, by four divers employed by an American diving contractor, their aim being to bring changes to an industry that treated them with contempt, offered low wages, and had no realistic health and safety regime.

Membership flourished, and in 1985 the Association was awarded their certificate, by the Certification Office for Trade Unions and Employers Associations, declaring the Association to be a recognised Independent Trade Union.

At the beginning of 1987, members of the Executive became engaged in a series of discussions with an organisation which would ultimately provide the PDA with a wealth of industrial experience, new development ideas, new standing, and long term security, and an agreement in principle was achieved between the PDA and AMPS, the Association of Management and Professional Staffs.

In 1989, a huge vote was cast in favour of the transfer of undertakings to AMPS, when it was agreed by all that the long-term security of the Association was paramount, and that its future members would benefit from having a professional organisation to look after its interests and welfare.

There are currently two unions that any diver can join. Amongst both of their extensive interests they deal with UK diver's onshore matters, and divers working abroad, and also with UK offshore matters, each to a greater or lesser degree, and it will be up to the individual diver to make a decision as to which union he might join, or indeed if he wants to join them both, or neither.

It is certainly highly recommended that he does join a union for the very many benefits that will accrue there from, not least of which is the legal backing that each individual will get in the event of an accident, in or out of the water if it is work related and, dare I say, death, when next of kin are helped and protected at this most vulnerable of times.

On a lighter note, within the union there are many advantages to be gained, not least in advice on investing your hard earned money, pensions, mortgages, Building Society loans and insurance, and the Professional Diver's Section of AMPS, an autonomous section of the AEEU, still professes to be 'Britain's most progressive and caring Union'.

Anyone employed in the diving industry is able to join the Diver's Section of AMPS which, as members of the Amalgamated Engineering and Electrical Union, are great believers in negotiation rather than confrontation, with industrial action very much a last resort. Their main aim is to secure improved pay and working conditions through regular discussions with employers, and union fees are very low considering the benefits.

First and foremost, here is a highly professional body to fight on the diver's behalf in pay negotiations and legal disputes, and in an industry where many are self-employed it is vital to have a body to provide support in any dispute. In addition, AMPS provides its members with an accidental death or injury policy, and will fight on any member's behalf on matters of safety, or in any disagreement with an employer. Without this backing, legal fees could prove prohibitive.

This particular Union's diver representative, Michael Cocks, who has vast experience of the diving industry, works hand in glove with the HSE, and concerns himself in the main with inshore diving conditions and divers, and has campaigned for over ten years on its behalf to bring safety conditions into line with those in the North Sea, as well as endeavouring to persuade the Association of Diving Contractors to introduce better pay and conditions. He has said that it is vital that Civil Diving companies are forced to follow a standard code of practice, and that the powers of and enforcement by the HSE are considerably strengthened.

At this time he is endeavouring to find out how British divers can get work in the United States and Canada, without emigrating there. He believes it possible, as mentioned in the text, that by doing a short course at one of the American diver training schools, work may be obtained over there, so it is worth keeping in touch with him. It's obviously wise, and in your own best interests, to sell your skills to the highest bidder!

The RMT, or to give it it's full title, the National Union of Rail, Maritime and Transport Workers, is basically a transport union and, though its main diver interests are directed offshore, does not have a diver looking after divers' interests within the union, as in the past. It does, however, have more than 1,000 trained representatives dedicated to looking after its broad spectrum of interests throughout Britain, and also has its own legal team to look after any matters concerning a member who needs representation. As well as negotiating fair pay and conditions for its membership, just as any other union, it deals all importantly with matters of safety and safe working practises. Other membership benefits, as with AMPS, cover death and accident representation; loss of earnings; income tax; pensions; and other financial services, and also professes to give you 'the best protection you are ever likely to get at work.'

I feel perfectly certain that both Unions will give the working diver the very best of help, advice, and protection from any kind of adversity relating to his employment, and probably unstintingly outside of it too, so it's entirely up to the individual which way he chooses to go, but he should certainly bear in mind that these unions do sterling work for lots of people who thought it could never happen to them so, whatever you do, don't go without one!

Addendum

Said previously to be the largest undeveloped oil-field in the North Sea, the Clair field (pages 1/2), west of Shetland, *discovered 24 years ago,* is now to be developed following recent (late 2001) approval by the Energy Minister Brian Wilson of a £M 650 plan to get the recoverable oil out and pumped to Shetland. Said to have deposits of around two billion barrels, the field is owned by a conglomerate of five of the world's largest oil companies, headed by British Petroleum, the major shareholder, and will employ more than 1,000 people. As previously stated by BP's Chief Executive Sir John Browne, 'investment in the North Sea will continue to rise this year', and already over £2 billion is earmarked for various projects.

Useful Addresses

Dealing with all matters in the UK connected with regulations relating to commercial divers and diving, diver certifications and medical requirements is: The Health and Safety Executive, Offshore Division, Rose Court, 2 Southwark Bridge, London. SE1 9HS. Tel: 020 7717 6000. Fax: 020 7717 6678.

(It should be noted that in the above context 'UK' does not apply to Northern Ireland, which has its own Health and Safety Act and Diving Regulations, but has no certificate scheme.)

The International Marine Contractors Association (IMCA) represents offshore, marine and underwater engineering companies. They have over 150 member companies engaged in all aspects of the offshore and other related industries, including many diving companies, and an up to date membership list may be obtained from:

Carlyle House, 235 Vauxhall Bridge Road, London, SW1V 1EJ. Tel: +44 20 7931 8935. Fax: +44 20 7931 8935. E-mail: imca@imca-int.com. Website: http://www.imca-int.com.

The Association of Diving Contractors represents those companies involved with inland or inshore diving operations in the UK and Ireland. A full list of members may be obtained from the office of the Secretary - Crawford Logan at:

The Association of Diving Contractors, 54 Morningfield Road, Aberdeen, AB15 4AQ. Tel: 01224 312721. Fax: 01224 323961.

The Professional Diver's Section of AMPS, The Association of Management and Professional Staffs, is the diver's union affiliated to the AEEU, the Amalgamated Engineering and Electrical Union, and deals mainly with divers employed in the UK inshore industry, but some offshore and overseas. Their representative is:

Michael Cocks, Flat 2, 32 Kensington Park Gardens, London, W11 2QS. Tel: 020 7727 8208. Fax: 020 7221 8117. E-mail: kelynack@freeuk.com.

The union of divers mainly connected with offshore matters, but with onshore also, is affiliated to the RMT, The National Union of Rail, Maritime and Transport Workers. Although they do not have a diver representing divers' interests at this time, they do have more than 1,000 trained representatives situated around the UK, and initial contact can be made at:

Unity House, 205 Euston Road, London, NW1 2BL. Tel: 020 7387 4771. Fax: 020 7387 4123. Website: www.rmt.org.uk

Diver Training Schools:

The Underwater Centre, Fort William, Inverness-shire, Scotland. PH3 6LZ. Tel: +44 1397 703786. Fax: +44 1397 704969.

Fort Bovisand Diver Training Limited, Fort Bovisand, Plymouth, Devon, PL9 OAB. Tel: 01752 408021. Fax: 01752 481952.

If you want to keep fully up to date with the latest underwater technology and related matters, the *Underwater Contractor International* magazine is published six times a year by Underwater World Publications Ltd, 55 High Street, Teddington, Middlesex, TW11 8HA. Tel: +44 (0)20 8943 4288. Fax: +44 (0)20 8943 4312. E-mail: enquiries@divermag.co.uk

ACKNOWLEDGEMENTS

I am deeply indebted to all of the following for the help and encouragement I have been given over the last year or so, as without that willing help and generous input the writing of this tribute would have taken a great deal longer in getting to press, and indeed may never have got there at all.

The Health and Safety Executive (Offshore Division, Diving Operations Strategy Team); British Petroleum Education Department; The Institute of Naval Medicine, Gosport, Hants; my twin brothers Barry (Blondie) Limbrick, BEM, and Michael; my wife Carole; Kevin Patience, FRGS; John Bevan, Editor of Underwater Contractor International magazine; Alan and Angela Cray; Martin Cooper; Tracey Everett; Margaret Wyett; Bert Weaver, my Web Wizard; Michael Cocks; Dave Saywell; The British Sub Aqua Club; Hunstanton Public Library, Norfolk; Great Yarmouth Public Library, Norfolk; The Stationery Office; Sheriff Court, Aberdeen; Norwich Combined Court Centre; Bill Brown; Jeff (Buck) Taylor; John Dadd, BEM; Linda Elder who edited the MS; and Richard Fitt my patient and helpful editor/publisher. Staatstoezicht op de Mijnen (State Supervision of Mines) Netherlands; Dagny Hysing-Dahl; translators Bjorn and Elaine Schmithuysen; The Norwegian Petroleum Directorate; The International Marine Contractors Association; The UK Offshore Operators Association; and The Association of Diving Contractors.

My thanks to Reader's Digest Association Ltd for their kind permission to reproduce information extracted from Reader's Digest Library of Modern Knowledge. Copyright 1978.

Special thanks to Commander S.A. "Jackie" Warner, M.B.E., D.S.C., former Chief Inspector of Diving at the Department of Energy and joint author with Fred Park (deceased) of 'Requiem For A Diver', and his publishers Brown, Son & Ferguson of Darnley Street, Glasgow, for their kind permission to use some finer detail from their book regarding diver fatalities. I even borrowed the word 'Requiem' to form part of my own book title, but I hope that Jackie will consider that act a compliment to his good choice of title for his own book as, for me, it is the very word that most aptly sums up what we should ask for in remembering those divers.

Thanks also to The Institute of Petroleum Library and their website (www.petroleum.co.uk) which holds what is probably the most comprehensive collection of published material on all aspects of the oil industry which is readily accessible in the United Kingdom.

"Crown Copyright is reproduced with the permission of The Controller of Her Majesty's Stationery Office" in regard to extracts from The Development of The Oil and Gas Resources of the United Kingdom 1999 URN/146.

Crown Copyright legislation is reproduced under the terms of Crown Copyright Policy Guidance issued by HMSO.

Information regarding the Piper Alpha Disaster and subsequent recommendations is reproduced from Volumes One and Two of 'The Public Enquiry Into The Piper Alpha Disaster'.

In regard to 'A Step Change in Safety', whilst every effort has been made to ensure the accuracy of the information contained in this publication, neither UKOOA, nor any of its members, will assume liability for any use made thereof. The article is reproduced by kind permission of the UK Offshore Operators Association.